NO WORRIES

A GUIDED JOURNAL TO HELP YOU
CALM ANXIETY, RELIEVE STRESS, AND
PRACTICE POSITIVE THINKING EACH DAY

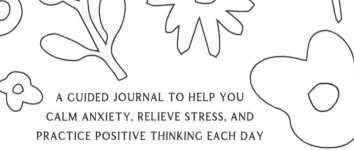

ISBN: 978-1952676000

Printed in U.S.A.

NO WORRIES

A GUIDED JOURNAL TO HELP YOU
CALM ANXIETY, RELIEVE STRESS, AND
PRACTICE POSITIVE THINKING EACH DAY

INTRODUCTION

Life can throw a lot of stress and worries your way. Sometimes they're self-generated, arising from your own personal feelings, fears, or actions. But other times they come from external forces outside your control, like politics, societal pressures, or social media. Either way, stress and worried thoughts can often make you feel like you're losing control, and when you feel that way, that's usually when anxiety starts to surface and overwhelm you.

If you suffer from anxiety, or struggle with anxious or worried thoughts, then you should first take comfort in knowing you aren't alone. Many people are battling anxiety these days. In fact, anxiety disorders affect 40 million adults in the United States age 18 and older each year.

Anxiety might be making you feel restless or panicked, but just by getting this journal, you have already made a positive step forward:

YOU HAVE ACKNOWLEDGED YOU STRUGGLE WITH ANXIETY AND WORRIED THOUGHTS AND THAT THEY'RE AFFECTING YOUR MENTAL HEALTH AND HAPPINESS.

YOU EMBRACED THE FACT THAT YOU NEED HELP AND WANT TO DO SOMETHING ABOUT IT,

YOU ACTED ON THAT DECISION.

Making the decision to take action is significant, so give yourself credit! Reducing anxiety is a process, and there is no one-size-fits-all roadmap to get there. However, this journal will fulfill the critical aspect of helping you plan, focus, and track your progress each day. It was designed as a 12-week journal because that is generally how long it takes to create meaningful lifestyle change.

It is universally recommended to find a therapist or counselor to help as well, since only a professional can uncover the root causes of your anxiety or stress and assist with creating the best plan for your unique needs. That said, the concepts in this journal are also universally accepted as part of the foundational work needed to cope with your anxiety so that you can start to feel better. Journaling your feelings, combating negative thoughts, and practicing mindfulness and gratitude are all part of building healthier habits, just like exercise, eating better, and sleep are essential as well.

This guided journal was designed to fit your needs and meet you where you are now. It is YOUR book to fill out how YOU want. You don't have to fill out every line; in fact, you can skip an entire section if it's not helpful. This isn't one of those "workbooks" that is only effective if you follow precise steps and don't skip any pages. No, this journal is the opposite. It is a primer, a guide, and a companion for your personal journey. So, let's get into what you'll find in this journal and some tips for how to use the various sections.

GETTING STARTED

The first part of this journal features the following four sections, which will help create a baseline for getting started:

SELF-CARE START-UP IDEAS : Since life presents one stressor after another, it's important to create a healthy foundation for day-to-day living so you can take good care of yourself. Anxiety and worries often arise because of things we can't control, but one thing you can start to control is how you care for yourself. On this page, you'll write down the things you want to do for self-care but haven't acted upon yet. Try not to make a list of negative things you want to eliminate from your life. Instead, make a list of positive things you want to add, even if they are ultimately replacing something negative. For example, don't say "I need to quit leaving the bed a mess," but instead write, "I want to make my bed in the morning because it'll help me accomplish something at the start of my day."

EMOTIONAL SUPPORT CHEAT SHEET : Whenever your thoughts start to spiral, it's so important to have people and things in your life that can ground you and remind you of what's good in your life. Exactly how it sounds, this cheat sheet will help you record the people and things that you know you can rely upon to make you feel better. That way, whenever you are feeling lost or struggling, you can come back to this list if you need someone or something to help center you and calm your nerves.

TRIGGER SOURCES : In this section, you will make a list of stress or anxiety triggers in your life and put them in objective terms for yourself, so you can begin to try and counteract them. Triggers of anxiety and stress are not always what the world would define as "rational." They can be simple or complex, tangible or only perceived. Big or small, there are no right answers. Whatever you are feeling is real to you!

MINDFULNESS MATTERS : Mindfulness really is a practice. You don't get "better" or "worse" at it, and it's not work that is ever finished or complete. Mindfulness is a critical component of a healthy self-care routine. Also, it is surprisingly simple! A therapist or counselor can give you additional insight that might help your specific needs, but this helpful reminder is beneficial for anyone.

USING YOUR JOURNAL

....

➤ DAILY ◄

THOUGHT LOG : This is a place to monitor the thoughts that are on your mind each day. Did something happen to make your thoughts start to spiral? What if you were to say it out loud: would it still feel rational or true? Positive or negative, use this space to pay attention to what flows through your mind and how it might be adding to your anxiety. Writing down your thoughts and worries can help you think through them and try to reframe them. For example:

WHAT WAS ON MY MIND TODAY : *My boss seemed upset with me because my project did not meet expectations. I must be a failure and she hates me. I'll probably be fired any day now. I'm the only one who screws up like this. I wish I could be like everyone else at work.*

HOW MIGHT I REFRAME THESE THOUGHTS? : *This was a super challenging project with a short schedule and reduced budget. I know everyone in my department has been struggling on this project. I'll learn from this and re-focus so we catch up next month.*

TRIGGER TRACKER : Since you already spent some valuable time identifying common triggers of stress and anxiety in your life, you can use this section to keep track of when they come up for you. What seems to bring them on, and how do you react? How might you learn how to react differently? Journaling about these moments and situations can help you reflect on what's causing them, so you can get to the root of the issue and work to shift your perspective or approach.

ACCOMPLISHMENTS/WINS : This section is about logging the moments—big and small—that make you feel good or proud each day. It might be as simple as noting that you were feeling tired or sad one afternoon, but then got up and went outside for a walk and felt much better afterward. The best part of feeling better is that it can start an upward spiral and help create even more positive moments in your life!

SELF-CARE REMINDER : Use this section as a daily check-in to keep track of whether you're taking basic steps to care for yourself each day. If you don't do them all, or slip up, that's totally fine. But treat this as a gentle reminder to do what's good for you.

DAILY GRATITUDE : Although "gratitude" isn't directly related to anxiety, it certainly helps to create positive, healthy thoughts and spend a little time each day reflecting on what you are grateful for in your life. Maybe you're grateful for a close friend, or your spouse or partner. Or maybe you're just grateful that the sky was blue, and that traffic was light on your way to the office. Remember, developing a gratitude practice isn't about only celebrating the big or tangible things in your life. It can be as small and simple as "I saw someone pick up a piece of litter today and throw it away. It made me happy and reminded me that other people care."

SOMETHING THAT MADE YOU HAPPY : What's one thing that lifted your spirits or made you smile? Even if it was just meeting a friendly dog while you were out in your neighborhood, that's enough! Remember to always look for the little moments of joy in life each day.

➤ WEEKLY ◀

FEAR-SETTING : Use this section to manage expectations or fears that arise each week. If you start to worry about something, break it down and think about the worst-case scenario, the best-case scenario, and the most likely scenario. For instance, if you say something you regret to a friend or family member and start to worry that they won't like you anymore, manage your fears and try to reflect on what a more realistic outcome might be.

HAPPY HABIT TRACKER : What healthy habits have you decided to incorporate into your routine? Go for a walk once a day? Eat a salad at lunch? Meditate every morning? Watch less TV, or spend less time on social media? Whatever it is, keep track of the habits you are trying to build, and how well you stick to them each week. (Some of these may come from the self-care start-up ideas page you completed before.) Staying on track will make it much easier for new habits to form and for them to become a natural part of your life.

THERAPY REFLECTIONS : If you're seeing a therapist or counselor, you can jot down notes from your meetings here. And even if you're not seeing a therapist, but are still making time for conversations with someone you love or trust, then you can use this space to document what you spoke to them about and how it made you feel. Intimate conversations — be it with a therapist, partner, or friend—can feel uncomfortable. That's natural because you are making yourself vulnerable and discussing things you likely don't talk about, which is a good thing! Treat this space in your journal as a place to process those discussions.

➤ MONTHLY ❰

MONTHLY PROGRESS CHECK-IN : At the end of every four weeks, take a few minutes to check in with yourself, look back at your daily and weekly pages, and journal about how you feel about them. Try to be objective, but fair to yourself here. You aren't expected to make huge steps forward every month. Try to think of the previous month from a high-level view, meaning you should think about how the month was on average or as a whole. You surely had good and bad days, but don't let either one override the others.

MEASURE YOUR SATISFACTION : During your monthly check-in, you can also "interview" yourself and think objectively about how you are feeling about different areas of your life. Rate how you feel without the pressure of having to justify your feelings or relate them back to any event or outside factor. If you feel sad or disappointed, then that's OK. Don't let your feelings about one area of your life inform how you feel about yourself overall. That's why this exercise is such a good thing: it can help you see the areas in your life where you are satisfied, giving you some perspective that things are probably going pretty well for you overall.

LET'S
GET
STARTED

SELF-CARE START-UP IDEAS:

"Self-care" relates to things big and small, as well as short and long-term. Both are important, but the key is to start with the small things. The big and long-term things will feel easy when the time comes.

"Taking time to care for yourself isn't selfish. It's a radical act of self-love."

START SMALL.

- ☑ Make my bed
- ☐ Make a cup of coffee/tea
- ☑ Take breaks from phone or social media
- ☐ _____
- ☐ _____

START MOVING.

- ☑ Go for a walk
- ☑ Stretch
- ☐ Get 15-30 minutes of natural light outside
- ☐ _____
- ☐ _____

START SOCIALIZING.

- ☐ Call or text a friend
- ☐ Visit a therapist
- ☑ Join a local group
- ☐ _____
- ☐ _____

START RELAXING.

- ☐ Watch my favorite TV show
- ☑ Listen to a podcast or music
- ☑ Read a book
- ☐ _____
- ☐ _____

EMOTIONAL SUPPORT
CHEAT SHEET:

Always remember that you are on a journey. You are not doing good or bad, and there will ALWAYS be some ups and downs. Refer to this "cheat sheet" any time you need someone or something to lift your spirits!

PEOPLE I TRUST FOR SUPPORT :

1	2	3
Kara	Doc	

MY VALUES :

_____

_____

_____

_____

_____

ACTIVITIES I ENJOY :

Air Soft
Books
Games

THING I LOVE
THE MOST:

My Wife
My frinds

FAVORITE
QUOTES:

You are not What you
were born but What
you have in yourself
to be —
What Man is a man
who does not make
the world better

TRIGGER SOURCES:

Log any emotional triggers that come to mind in each of these categories.

PEOPLE :	PLACES :
Dad Mom Brothers Kavo Mr Ray mis Ray	Work Home

THINGS :	SITUATIONS :
Sex Bill's	

EMOTIONAL STATES :	OTHER :

Now, think about ways you can overcome these triggers. It could be as simple as taking a deep breath and walking away. You might also need to pre-plan for acceptance of things you cannot control, adjusting how you perceive those triggers, or having a way to distract yourself when needed.

MINDFULNESS MATTERS:

Finding a few minutes to pause and rest your mind is essential for clearing out cluttered thoughts and bringing you back to the here and now. Remember: Mindfulness is a PRACTICE. Not an accomplishment! It's something you have to work on a little bit each day.

MINDFULNESS IS :
....

Being aware of oneself and one's surroundings, no matter the state

Being present, non-judgmental, and accepting

Focusing on sensory observations (what you hear, smell, feel, etc.) and over-analytical observations (who, why, how, etc.)

MINDFULNESS ISN'T :
....

A silencing of the mind where you are

Not letting any thoughts creep in, or about controlling or subduing negative thoughts or behaviors

A scheduled activity that must be done only in calm and peaceful settings

---

HOW TO PRACTICE MINDFULNESS :

1. Set aside a few minutes. Find a quiet, comfortable place to sit. Close your eyes and bring your focus towards yourself.

2. Notice any physical sensations you may be feeling, scanning your body from head to toe.

3. Take slow, deep breaths. Feel each breath fill your body.

4. Your mind will inevitably begin to wander. That's OK! Allow your mind to wander for a bit before gently guiding your focus back to your breathing.

5. Continue for as long as you desire.

WEEK 1:

DATE 1/5/21

OVERALL MOOD:

(HAPPY) (ENERGETIC) (CALM) (STRESSED) (SAD) (TIRED)

➤ THOUGHT LOG: ◀

WHAT WAS ON MY MIND TODAY? im upset with my self because I mest up and mit have goten sick

HOW MIGHT I REFRAME THOSE THOUGHTS? I dont Know

➤ TRIGGER TRACKER: ◀

DID SOMETHING TRIGGER MY ANXIETY TODAY? Kana yelld at my she was well within her rite i relle mest up

HOW DID I RESPOND? I got up set and locked up and then yelld back

ACCOMPLISHMENTS/WINS:

1 I Drill A hole in the garbig can

2 went to therapy

3

SELF-CARE:

☐ DID I SLEEP WELL?
No

☐ DID I GET EXERCISE?
No

☐ DID I GET FRESH AIR?
yes

☐ DID I MEDITATE?
No

☐ DID I EAT NOURISHING FOODS? No

DAILY GRATITUDE:

1. MX wife
2. Not bing sick
3.
4.
5.

SOMETHING THAT MADE ME HAPPY TODAY:

I gave Some kids toys

DATE 1/6/21

OVERALL MOOD:

(HAPPY)　(ENERGETIC)　(CALM)　(STRESSED)　(SAD X)　(TIRED X)

➤ THOUGHT LOG: ◄

WHAT WAS ON MY MIND TODAY? All the thing's
I have done. Bad in my life and
how much I have failed at life

HOW MIGHT I REFRAME THOSE THOUGHTS? Try to be a
Beter man and move forward

➤ TRIGGER TRACKER: ◄

DID SOMETHING TRIGGER MY ANXIETY TODAY? Doing this
Book

HOW DID I RESPOND? I got upset and
moped all day

ACCOMPLISHMENTS/WINS:

1	I made Supe

2	I went Back to work

3	I talked to Kara about how i fellt

SELF-CARE:

- ● DID I SLEEP WELL?
- ☐ DID I GET EXERCISE?
- ● DID I GET FRESH AIR?
- ☐ DID I MEDITATE?
- ● DID I EAT NOURISHING FOODS?

DAILY GRATITUDE:

1. Kara
2.
3.
4.
5.

SOMETHING THAT MADE ME HAPPY TODAY:

how much Kara tride to help me it showed me Just how much she loves me.

DATE 1/7/21

OVERALL MOOD:

(HAPPY) (ENERGETIC) (CALM) (STRESSED X) (SAD X) (TIRED X)

➤ THOUGHT LOG: ◄

WHAT WAS ON MY MIND TODAY? My Boss and me trying to get a new Jod

HOW MIGHT I REFRAME THOSE THOUGHTS? try to look move to the povotiev

➤ TRIGGER TRACKER: ◄

DID SOMETHING TRIGGER MY ANXIETY TODAY? My boss

HOW DID I RESPOND? I got Sad Mad and Stressed

ACCOMPLISHMENTS/WINS:

1 got A Lot of Stuf done At work

2 Made Good food

3

SELF-CARE:

☐ DID I SLEEP WELL?

☐ DID I GET EXERCISE?

☑ DID I GET FRESH AIR?

☐ DID I MEDITATE?

☑ DID I EAT NOURISHING FOODS?

DAILY GRATITUDE:

1. My wife

2.

3.

4.

5.

**SOMETHING THAT
MADE ME HAPPY TODAY:**

I got to get out More

DATE 1/8/21

OVERALL MOOD:

(HAPPY) (ENERGETIC X) (CALM) (STRESSED) (SAD X) (TIRED)

> **THOUGHT LOG:** <

WHAT WAS ON MY MIND TODAY? Not a Lot
at first but Kara Sed Somthings
That made me Sad

HOW MIGHT I REFRAME THOSE THOUGHTS? Look at
what She Said as her trying
to move ford

> **TRIGGER TRACKER:** <

DID SOMETHING TRIGGER MY ANXIETY TODAY? Karo

HOW DID I RESPOND? I got Sad But we
talked It out

ACCOMPLISHMENTS/WINS:

1	2	3
got A l ot Done	Didint Holb Back my fellings	

SELF-CARE:

- ☐ DID I SLEEP WELL?
- ☑ DID I GET EXERCISE?
- ☑ DID I GET FRESH AIR?
- ☐ DID I MEDITATE?
- ☑ DID I EAT NOURISHING FOODS?

DAILY GRATITUDE:

1. GoD
2. Kara
3. Doc
4.
5.

SOMETHING THAT MADE ME HAPPY TODAY:

I got Make Stake

DATE V9/21

OVERALL MOOD:

(HAPPY ⨯) (ENERGETIC ⨯) (CALM) (STRESSED) (SAD ⨯) (TIRED ⨯)

➤ THOUGHT LOG: ◄

WHAT WAS ON MY MIND TODAY? Kavas Bro
and how he is doing stuff
that Mite hurt him

HOW MIGHT I REFRAME THOSE THOUGHTS? I dont
Know

➤ TRIGGER TRACKER: ◄

DID SOMETHING TRIGGER MY ANXIETY TODAY? Not
Relly

HOW DID I RESPOND? good

ACCOMPLISHMENTS/WINS:

1 Me and Kara got A lloT Done At the Reno

2

3

SELF-CARE:

☐ DID I SLEEP WELL?

☑ DID I GET EXERCISE?

☑ DID I GET FRESH AIR?

☑ DID I MEDITATE?

☑ DID I EAT NOURISHING FOODS?

DAILY GRATITUDE:

1. Kara
2. Kara's Dad
3. Kara's mom
4. Doc
5.

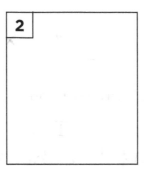

SOMETHING THAT
MADE ME HAPPY TODAY:

Playing Games With the famaly

DATE 1/10/21

OVERALL MOOD:

HAPPY ❌ ENERGETIC CALM STRESSED ❌ SAD TIRED ❌

➤ **THOUGHT LOG:** ◀

WHAT WAS ON MY MIND TODAY? I was really worried about Kara's Bro and how he was doing

HOW MIGHT I REFRAME THOSE THOUGHTS? try to help if I can

➤ **TRIGGER TRACKER:** ◀

DID SOMETHING TRIGGER MY ANXIETY TODAY? My boss got mad at me for somthing stupid and not a prodlom

HOW DID I RESPOND? I was good and wen I left I talked to Kara

DAY: 6

ACCOMPLISHMENTS/WINS:

1	2	3
Worked on the New Home	Fixed the TV	Did some of my PW for Kara

SELF-CARE:

- [ ] DID I SLEEP WELL?
- [x] DID I GET EXERCISE?
- [x] DID I GET FRESH AIR?
- [x] DID I MEDITATE?
- [x] DID I EAT NOURISHING FOODS?

DAILY GRATITUDE:

1. Kard
2. my frinds
3. Having a Home
4.
5.

SOMETHING THAT MADE ME HAPPY TODAY:

Spending the morning in bed wiht Kara

DATE 1/11/21

OVERALL MOOD:

(HAPPY) (ENERGETIC) (CALM) (STRESSED X) (SAD X) (TIRED X)

➤ THOUGHT LOG: ◄

WHAT WAS ON MY MIND TODAY? Work and my famaly

HOW MIGHT I REFRAME THOSE THOUGHTS? trye not to think abat it

➤ TRIGGER TRACKER: ◄

DID SOMETHING TRIGGER MY ANXIETY TODAY? work and famaly

HOW DID I RESPOND? I got sad and stressed

ACCOMPLISHMENTS/WINS:

1	2	3
nothing	Nothing	

SELF-CARE:

☒ DID I SLEEP WELL?
No

☐ DID I GET EXERCISE?
Yes

☐ DID I GET FRESH AIR?
Yes

☐ DID I MEDITATE?
No

☐ DID I EAT NOURISHING FOODS? No

DAILY GRATITUDE:

1. Kard
2.
3.
4.
5.

SOMETHING THAT MADE ME HAPPY TODAY:

I relley wasent

WEEKLY FEAR-SETTING:

WHAT AM I WORRIED ABOUT RIGHT NOW? Work and
What Will hapen wene I leve

HOW LIKELY IS IT FOR THIS TO ACTUALLY OCCUR? THINK OF YOUR
PAST EXPERIENCES AND WRITE ANY EXAMPLES HERE. Vere

WHAT'S THE WORST-CASE SCENARIO?

I will Lous my New Job and
the place I live

% CHANCE OF THAT HAPPENING? 30

WHAT'S THE BEST-CASE SCENARIO?

evrething is ok and We rae still
good frinds

% CHANCE OF THAT HAPPENING? 79

WHAT'S THE MOST LIKELY SCENARIO?

The Ray's drent Happy bat want
the best for me. But thay still
get upset with me

% CHANCE OF THAT HAPPENING? _____

HAPPY HABIT TRACKER:

HABIT TRACKER:	S	M	T	W	T	F	S
	□	□	□	□	□	□	□
	□	□	□	□	□	□	□
	□	□	□	□	□	□	□
	□	□	□	□	□	□	□
	□	□	□	□	□	□	□
	□	□	□	□	□	□	□
	□	□	□	□	□	□	□
	□	□	□	□	□	□	□
	□	□	□	□	□	□	□
	□	□	□	□	□	□	□
	□	□	□	□	□	□	□
	□	□	□	□	□	□	□
	□	□	□	□	□	□	□
	□	□	□	□	□	□	□
	□	□	□	□	□	□	□
	□	□	□	□	□	□	□

THERAPY REFLECTIONS:

I didin't go thi week

TOPIC WE DISCUSSED:	HOW I FEEL ABOUT IT:

TAKEAWAYS:	FOR NEXT TIME:

WEEK 2:

DATE 1/19/21

OVERALL MOOD:

(HAPPY) (ENERGETIC) (CALM X) (STRESSED 🔨) (SAD) (TIRED)

➤ THOUGHT LOG: ◄

WHAT WAS ON MY MIND TODAY? I Was Woried
abut my new Job

HOW MIGHT I REFRAME THOSE THOUGHTS? try to see
the good and not the bad

➤ TRIGGER TRACKER: ◄

DID SOMETHING TRIGGER MY ANXIETY TODAY? Not Vally

HOW DID I RESPOND?

ACCOMPLISHMENTS/WINS:

1 got A lot done At Work

2 Fixtd MY tent

3

SELF-CARE:

☑ DID I SLEEP WELL?

☑ DID I GET EXERCISE?

☑ DID I GET FRESH AIR?

☑ DID I MEDITATE?

☐ DID I EAT NOURISHING FOODS?

DAILY GRATITUDE:

1. Kard

2. Doc

3. Tomas

4. the Ray's

5.

SOMETHING THAT MADE ME HAPPY TODAY:

I Love spending time with Kard

DATE 1/20/21

OVERALL MOOD:

(HAPPY) X (ENERGETIC) X (CALM) (STRESSED) X (SAD) (TIRED) X

➤ THOUGHT LOG: ◄

WHAT WAS ON MY MIND TODAY? Just life
and what all Hapend last year
and how it was changd my life
both good and bad

HOW MIGHT I REFRAME THOSE THOUGHTS? try to look
at it as a hole and not Jast
the good and bad

➤ TRIGGER TRACKER: ◄

DID SOMETHING TRIGGER MY ANXIETY TODAY? Not relly

HOW DID I RESPOND?

ACCOMPLISHMENTS/WINS:

1	2	3
got the RAX's bed fixed up		

SELF-CARE:

- ☐ DID I SLEEP WELL?
- ☑ DID I GET EXERCISE?
- ☑ DID I GET FRESH AIR?
- ☑ DID I MEDITATE?
- ☐ DID I EAT NOURISHING FOODS?

DAILY GRATITUDE:

1. Kara
2. Doc
3. Grant
4. Hunter
5.

SOMETHING THAT MADE ME HAPPY TODAY:

Thinking about going Camping With Kara

DATE _____

OVERALL MOOD:

(HAPPY) (ENERGETIC) (CALM) (STRESSED) (SAD) (TIRED)

❯ THOUGHT LOG: ❮

WHAT WAS ON MY MIND TODAY? _____

_____

_____

_____

HOW MIGHT I REFRAME THOSE THOUGHTS? _____

_____

_____

_____

❯ TRIGGER TRACKER: ❮

DID SOMETHING TRIGGER MY ANXIETY TODAY? _____

_____

_____

_____

HOW DID I RESPOND? _____

_____

_____

_____

DAY: 3

ACCOMPLISHMENTS/WINS:

1	2	3

SELF-CARE:

- ☐ DID I SLEEP WELL?
- ☐ DID I GET EXERCISE?
- ☐ DID I GET FRESH AIR?
- ☐ DID I MEDITATE?
- ☐ DID I EAT NOURISHING FOODS?

DAILY GRATITUDE:

1. _____
2. _____
3. _____
4. _____
5. _____

SOMETHING THAT
MADE ME HAPPY TODAY:

DATE _____

OVERALL MOOD:

(HAPPY) (ENERGETIC) (CALM) (STRESSED) (SAD) (TIRED)

➤ THOUGHT LOG: ◀

WHAT WAS ON MY MIND TODAY? _____

_____

_____

_____

HOW MIGHT I REFRAME THOSE THOUGHTS? _____

_____

_____

_____

➤ TRIGGER TRACKER: ◀

DID SOMETHING TRIGGER MY ANXIETY TODAY? _____

_____

_____

_____

HOW DID I RESPOND? _____

_____

_____

_____

DAY: 4

ACCOMPLISHMENTS/WINS:

1	2	3

SELF-CARE:

☐ DID I SLEEP WELL?

☐ DID I GET EXERCISE?

☐ DID I GET FRESH AIR?

☐ DID I MEDITATE?

☐ DID I EAT NOURISHING
FOODS?

DAILY GRATITUDE:

1. _____

2. _____

3. _____

4. _____

5. _____

SOMETHING THAT
MADE ME HAPPY TODAY:

DATE_____

OVERALL MOOD:

(HAPPY) (ENERGETIC) (CALM) (STRESSED) (SAD) (TIRED)

❯ THOUGHT LOG: ❮

WHAT WAS ON MY MIND TODAY? _____
_____
_____
_____

HOW MIGHT I REFRAME THOSE THOUGHTS? _____
_____
_____
_____
_____

❯ TRIGGER TRACKER: ❮

DID SOMETHING TRIGGER MY ANXIETY TODAY? _____
_____
_____
_____

HOW DID I RESPOND? _____
_____
_____
_____

DAY: 5

ACCOMPLISHMENTS/WINS:

1	2	3

SELF-CARE:

- ☐ DID I SLEEP WELL?
- ☐ DID I GET EXERCISE?
- ☐ DID I GET FRESH AIR?
- ☐ DID I MEDITATE?
- ☐ DID I EAT NOURISHING FOODS?

DAILY GRATITUDE:

1. _____
2. _____
3. _____
4. _____
5. _____

SOMETHING THAT
MADE ME HAPPY TODAY:

DATE _____

OVERALL MOOD:

(HAPPY)   (ENERGETIC)   (CALM)   (STRESSED)   (SAD)   (TIRED)

❯ THOUGHT LOG: ❮

WHAT WAS ON MY MIND TODAY? _____

_____

_____

_____

HOW MIGHT I REFRAME THOSE THOUGHTS? _____

_____

_____

_____

❯ TRIGGER TRACKER: ❮

DID SOMETHING TRIGGER MY ANXIETY TODAY? _____

_____

_____

_____

HOW DID I RESPOND? _____

_____

_____

_____

DAY: 6

ACCOMPLISHMENTS/WINS:

1	2	3

SELF-CARE:

☐ DID I SLEEP WELL?

☐ DID I GET EXERCISE?

☐ DID I GET FRESH AIR?

☐ DID I MEDITATE?

☐ DID I EAT NOURISHING
   FOODS?

DAILY GRATITUDE:

1. _____

2. _____

3. _____

4. _____

5. _____

SOMETHING THAT
MADE ME HAPPY TODAY:

DATE _____

OVERALL MOOD:

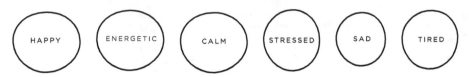

(HAPPY) (ENERGETIC) (CALM) (STRESSED) (SAD) (TIRED)

❯ THOUGHT LOG: ❮

WHAT WAS ON MY MIND TODAY? _____

_____

_____

_____

_____

HOW MIGHT I REFRAME THOSE THOUGHTS? _____

_____

_____

_____

_____

❯ TRIGGER TRACKER: ❮

DID SOMETHING TRIGGER MY ANXIETY TODAY? _____

_____

_____

_____

_____

HOW DID I RESPOND? _____

_____

_____

_____

_____

DAY: 7

ACCOMPLISHMENTS/WINS:

1	2	3

SELF-CARE:

☐ DID I SLEEP WELL?

☐ DID I GET EXERCISE?

☐ DID I GET FRESH AIR?

☐ DID I MEDITATE?

☐ DID I EAT NOURISHING FOODS?

DAILY GRATITUDE:

1. _____

2. _____

3. _____

4. _____

5. _____

SOMETHING THAT MADE ME HAPPY TODAY:

WEEKLY FEAR-SETTING:

WHAT AM I WORRIED ABOUT RIGHT NOW? _____

_____

_____

_____

HOW LIKELY IS IT FOR THIS TO ACTUALLY OCCUR? THINK OF YOUR
PAST EXPERIENCES AND WRITE ANY EXAMPLES HERE. _____

_____

_____

_____

WHAT'S THE WORST-CASE SCENARIO?

% CHANCE OF THAT HAPPENING? _____

WHAT'S THE BEST-CASE SCENARIO?

% CHANCE OF THAT HAPPENING? _____

WHAT'S THE MOST LIKELY SCENARIO?

% CHANCE OF THAT HAPPENING? _____

HAPPY HABIT TRACKER:

HABIT TRACKER:	S	M	T	W	T	F	S
	□	□	□	□	□	□	□
	□	□	□	□	□	□	□
	□	□	□	□	□	□	□
	□	□	□	□	□	□	□
	□	□	□	□	□	□	□
	□	□	□	□	□	□	□
	□	□	□	□	□	□	□
	□	□	□	□	□	□	□
	□	□	□	□	□	□	□
	□	□	□	□	□	□	□
	□	□	□	□	□	□	□
	□	□	□	□	□	□	□
	□	□	□	□	□	□	□
	□	□	□	□	□	□	□
	□	□	□	□	□	□	□
	□	□	□	□	□	□	□

THERAPY REFLECTIONS:

TOPIC WE DISCUSSED:

HOW I FEEL ABOUT IT:

TAKEAWAYS:

FOR NEXT TIME:

WEEK 3:

DATE_____

OVERALL MOOD:

(HAPPY) (ENERGETIC) (CALM) (STRESSED) (SAD) (TIRED)

❯ THOUGHT LOG: ❮

WHAT WAS ON MY MIND TODAY? _____
_____
_____
_____

HOW MIGHT I REFRAME THOSE THOUGHTS? _____
_____
_____
_____

❯ TRIGGER TRACKER: ❮

DID SOMETHING TRIGGER MY ANXIETY TODAY? _____
_____
_____
_____

HOW DID I RESPOND? _____
_____
_____
_____

DAY: 1

ACCOMPLISHMENTS/WINS:

1	2	3

SELF-CARE:

☐ DID I SLEEP WELL?

☐ DID I GET EXERCISE?

☐ DID I GET FRESH AIR?

☐ DID I MEDITATE?

☐ DID I EAT NOURISHING
FOODS?

DAILY GRATITUDE:

1. _____

2. _____

3. _____

4. _____

5. _____

SOMETHING THAT
MADE ME HAPPY TODAY:

DATE _____

OVERALL MOOD:

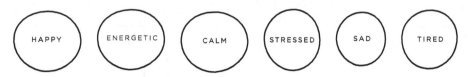

(HAPPY) (ENERGETIC) (CALM) (STRESSED) (SAD) (TIRED)

❯ THOUGHT LOG: ❮

WHAT WAS ON MY MIND TODAY? _____
_____
_____
_____
_____

HOW MIGHT I REFRAME THOSE THOUGHTS? _____
_____
_____
_____
_____

❯ TRIGGER TRACKER: ❮

DID SOMETHING TRIGGER MY ANXIETY TODAY? _____
_____
_____
_____
_____

HOW DID I RESPOND? _____
_____
_____
_____
_____

ACCOMPLISHMENTS/WINS:

1	2	3

SELF-CARE:

☐ DID I SLEEP WELL?

☐ DID I GET EXERCISE?

☐ DID I GET FRESH AIR?

☐ DID I MEDITATE?

☐ DID I EAT NOURISHING
   FOODS?

DAILY GRATITUDE:

1. _____

2. _____

3. _____

4. _____

5. _____

SOMETHING THAT
MADE ME HAPPY TODAY:

DATE _____

OVERALL MOOD:

(HAPPY) (ENERGETIC) (CALM) (STRESSED) (SAD) (TIRED)

❯ THOUGHT LOG: ❮

WHAT WAS ON MY MIND TODAY? _____

_____

_____

_____

HOW MIGHT I REFRAME THOSE THOUGHTS? _____

_____

_____

_____

❯ TRIGGER TRACKER: ❮

DID SOMETHING TRIGGER MY ANXIETY TODAY? _____

_____

_____

_____

HOW DID I RESPOND? _____

_____

_____

_____

DAY: 3

ACCOMPLISHMENTS/WINS:

1

2

3

SELF-CARE:

☐ DID I SLEEP WELL?

☐ DID I GET EXERCISE?

☐ DID I GET FRESH AIR?

☐ DID I MEDITATE?

☐ DID I EAT NOURISHING
   FOODS?

DAILY GRATITUDE:

1. _____

2. _____

3. _____

4. _____

5. _____

SOMETHING THAT
MADE ME HAPPY TODAY:

DATE _____

OVERALL MOOD:

HAPPY   ENERGETIC   CALM   STRESSED   SAD   TIRED

➤ THOUGHT LOG: ❰

WHAT WAS ON MY MIND TODAY? _____

_____

_____

_____

HOW MIGHT I REFRAME THOSE THOUGHTS? _____

_____

_____

_____

➤ TRIGGER TRACKER: ❰

DID SOMETHING TRIGGER MY ANXIETY TODAY? _____

_____

_____

_____

HOW DID I RESPOND? _____

_____

_____

_____

ACCOMPLISHMENTS/WINS:

1

2

3

SELF-CARE:

☐ DID I SLEEP WELL?

☐ DID I GET EXERCISE?

☐ DID I GET FRESH AIR?

☐ DID I MEDITATE?

☐ DID I EAT NOURISHING
FOODS?

DAILY GRATITUDE:

1. _____

2. _____

3. _____

4. _____

5. _____

SOMETHING THAT
MADE ME HAPPY TODAY:

DATE _____

OVERALL MOOD:

(HAPPY) (ENERGETIC) (CALM) (STRESSED) (SAD) (TIRED)

❯ THOUGHT LOG: ❮

WHAT WAS ON MY MIND TODAY? _____
_____
_____
_____

HOW MIGHT I REFRAME THOSE THOUGHTS? _____
_____
_____
_____
_____

❯ TRIGGER TRACKER: ❮

DID SOMETHING TRIGGER MY ANXIETY TODAY? _____
_____
_____
_____

HOW DID I RESPOND? _____
_____
_____
_____
_____

ACCOMPLISHMENTS/WINS:

1	2	3

SELF-CARE:

☐ DID I SLEEP WELL?

☐ DID I GET EXERCISE?

☐ DID I GET FRESH AIR?

☐ DID I MEDITATE?

☐ DID I EAT NOURISHING FOODS?

DAILY GRATITUDE:

1. _____

2. _____

3. _____

4. _____

5. _____

SOMETHING THAT
MADE ME HAPPY TODAY:

DATE _____

OVERALL MOOD:

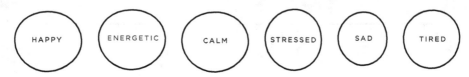

(HAPPY) (ENERGETIC) (CALM) (STRESSED) (SAD) (TIRED)

❯ THOUGHT LOG: ❮

WHAT WAS ON MY MIND TODAY? _____

_____

_____

_____

HOW MIGHT I REFRAME THOSE THOUGHTS? _____

_____

_____

_____

_____

❯ TRIGGER TRACKER: ❮

DID SOMETHING TRIGGER MY ANXIETY TODAY? _____

_____

_____

_____

HOW DID I RESPOND? _____

_____

_____

_____

ACCOMPLISHMENTS/WINS:

1	2	3

SELF-CARE:

- ☐ DID I SLEEP WELL?
- ☐ DID I GET EXERCISE?
- ☐ DID I GET FRESH AIR?
- ☐ DID I MEDITATE?
- ☐ DID I EAT NOURISHING FOODS?

DAILY GRATITUDE:

1. _____
2. _____
3. _____
4. _____
5. _____

SOMETHING THAT
MADE ME HAPPY TODAY:

DATE _____

OVERALL MOOD:

(HAPPY) (ENERGETIC) (CALM) (STRESSED) (SAD) (TIRED)

➤ THOUGHT LOG: ◄

WHAT WAS ON MY MIND TODAY? _____

_____

_____

_____

HOW MIGHT I REFRAME THOSE THOUGHTS? _____

_____

_____

_____

_____

➤ TRIGGER TRACKER: ◄

DID SOMETHING TRIGGER MY ANXIETY TODAY? _____

_____

_____

_____

HOW DID I RESPOND? _____

_____

_____

_____

_____

DAY: 7

ACCOMPLISHMENTS/WINS:

1	2	3

SELF-CARE:

- ☐ DID I SLEEP WELL?
- ☐ DID I GET EXERCISE?
- ☐ DID I GET FRESH AIR?
- ☐ DID I MEDITATE?
- ☐ DID I EAT NOURISHING FOODS?

DAILY GRATITUDE:

1. _____
2. _____
3. _____
4. _____
5. _____

SOMETHING THAT
MADE ME HAPPY TODAY:

WEEKLY FEAR-SETTING:

WHAT AM I WORRIED ABOUT RIGHT NOW? _____

_____

_____

_____

HOW LIKELY IS IT FOR THIS TO ACTUALLY OCCUR? THINK OF YOUR
PAST EXPERIENCES AND WRITE ANY EXAMPLES HERE. _____

_____

_____

_____

WHAT'S THE WORST-CASE SCENARIO?

% CHANCE OF THAT HAPPENING? _____

WHAT'S THE BEST-CASE SCENARIO?

% CHANCE OF THAT HAPPENING? _____

WHAT'S THE MOST LIKELY SCENARIO?

% CHANCE OF THAT HAPPENING? _____

HAPPY HABIT TRACKER:

HABIT TRACKER:	S	M	T	W	T	F	S
	☐	☐	☐	☐	☐	☐	☐
	☐	☐	☐	☐	☐	☐	☐
	☐	☐	☐	☐	☐	☐	☐
	☐	☐	☐	☐	☐	☐	☐
	☐	☐	☐	☐	☐	☐	☐
	☐	☐	☐	☐	☐	☐	☐
	☐	☐	☐	☐	☐	☐	☐
	☐	☐	☐	☐	☐	☐	☐
	☐	☐	☐	☐	☐	☐	☐
	☐	☐	☐	☐	☐	☐	☐
	☐	☐	☐	☐	☐	☐	☐
	☐	☐	☐	☐	☐	☐	☐
	☐	☐	☐	☐	☐	☐	☐
	☐	☐	☐	☐	☐	☐	☐
	☐	☐	☐	☐	☐	☐	☐
	☐	☐	☐	☐	☐	☐	☐

THERAPY REFLECTIONS:

TOPIC WE DISCUSSED:	HOW I FEEL ABOUT IT:

TAKEAWAYS:	FOR NEXT TIME:

WEEK 4:

DATE _____

OVERALL MOOD:

(HAPPY) (ENERGETIC) (CALM) (STRESSED) (SAD) (TIRED)

❯ THOUGHT LOG: ❮

WHAT WAS ON MY MIND TODAY? _____
_____
_____
_____

HOW MIGHT I REFRAME THOSE THOUGHTS? _____
_____
_____
_____

❯ TRIGGER TRACKER: ❮

DID SOMETHING TRIGGER MY ANXIETY TODAY? _____
_____
_____
_____

HOW DID I RESPOND? _____
_____
_____
_____

DAY: 1

ACCOMPLISHMENTS/WINS:

1	2	3

SELF-CARE:

☐ DID I SLEEP WELL?

☐ DID I GET EXERCISE?

☐ DID I GET FRESH AIR?

☐ DID I MEDITATE?

☐ DID I EAT NOURISHING FOODS?

DAILY GRATITUDE:

1. _____

2. _____

3. _____

4. _____

5. _____

**SOMETHING THAT
MADE ME HAPPY TODAY:**

DATE _____

OVERALL MOOD:

(HAPPY) (ENERGETIC) (CALM) (STRESSED) (SAD) (TIRED)

➤ THOUGHT LOG: ◀

WHAT WAS ON MY MIND TODAY? _____

_____

_____

_____

HOW MIGHT I REFRAME THOSE THOUGHTS? _____

_____

_____

_____

_____

➤ TRIGGER TRACKER: ◀

DID SOMETHING TRIGGER MY ANXIETY TODAY? _____

_____

_____

_____

HOW DID I RESPOND? _____

_____

_____

_____

_____

DAY: 2

ACCOMPLISHMENTS/WINS:

1

2

3

SELF-CARE:

☐ DID I SLEEP WELL?

☐ DID I GET EXERCISE?

☐ DID I GET FRESH AIR?

☐ DID I MEDITATE?

☐ DID I EAT NOURISHING FOODS?

DAILY GRATITUDE:

1. _____

2. _____

3. _____

4. _____

5. _____

SOMETHING THAT
MADE ME HAPPY TODAY:

DATE _____

OVERALL MOOD:

(HAPPY)　(ENERGETIC)　(CALM)　(STRESSED)　(SAD)　(TIRED)

➤ THOUGHT LOG: ❰

WHAT WAS ON MY MIND TODAY? _____
_____
_____
_____

HOW MIGHT I REFRAME THOSE THOUGHTS? _____
_____
_____
_____

➤ TRIGGER TRACKER: ❰

DID SOMETHING TRIGGER MY ANXIETY TODAY? _____
_____
_____
_____

HOW DID I RESPOND? _____
_____
_____
_____

ACCOMPLISHMENTS/WINS:

1	2	3

SELF-CARE:

☐ DID I SLEEP WELL?

☐ DID I GET EXERCISE?

☐ DID I GET FRESH AIR?

☐ DID I MEDITATE?

☐ DID I EAT NOURISHING FOODS?

DAILY GRATITUDE:

1. _____

2. _____

3. _____

4. _____

5. _____

SOMETHING THAT
MADE ME HAPPY TODAY:

DATE _____

OVERALL MOOD:

(HAPPY) (ENERGETIC) (CALM) (STRESSED) (SAD) (TIRED)

❯ THOUGHT LOG: ❮

WHAT WAS ON MY MIND TODAY? _____
_____
_____
_____

HOW MIGHT I REFRAME THOSE THOUGHTS? _____
_____
_____
_____

❯ TRIGGER TRACKER: ❮

DID SOMETHING TRIGGER MY ANXIETY TODAY? _____
_____
_____
_____

HOW DID I RESPOND? _____
_____
_____
_____

ACCOMPLISHMENTS/WINS:

1	2	3

SELF-CARE:

☐ DID I SLEEP WELL?

☐ DID I GET EXERCISE?

☐ DID I GET FRESH AIR?

☐ DID I MEDITATE?

☐ DID I EAT NOURISHING FOODS?

DAILY GRATITUDE:

1. _____

2. _____

3. _____

4. _____

5. _____

SOMETHING THAT
MADE ME HAPPY TODAY:

DATE _____

OVERALL MOOD:

(HAPPY)   (ENERGETIC)   (CALM)   (STRESSED)   (SAD)   (TIRED)

➤ THOUGHT LOG: ➤

WHAT WAS ON MY MIND TODAY? _____
_____
_____
_____

HOW MIGHT I REFRAME THOSE THOUGHTS? _____
_____
_____
_____

➤ TRIGGER TRACKER: ➤

DID SOMETHING TRIGGER MY ANXIETY TODAY? _____
_____
_____
_____

HOW DID I RESPOND? _____
_____
_____
_____

ACCOMPLISHMENTS/WINS:

1	2	3

SELF-CARE:

☐ DID I SLEEP WELL?

☐ DID I GET EXERCISE?

☐ DID I GET FRESH AIR?

☐ DID I MEDITATE?

☐ DID I EAT NOURISHING FOODS?

DAILY GRATITUDE:

1. _____

2. _____

3. _____

4. _____

5. _____

SOMETHING THAT MADE ME HAPPY TODAY:

DATE _____

OVERALL MOOD:

(HAPPY) (ENERGETIC) (CALM) (STRESSED) (SAD) (TIRED)

❯ THOUGHT LOG: ❮

WHAT WAS ON MY MIND TODAY? _____

_____

_____

_____

_____

HOW MIGHT I REFRAME THOSE THOUGHTS? _____

_____

_____

_____

_____

❯ TRIGGER TRACKER: ❮

DID SOMETHING TRIGGER MY ANXIETY TODAY? _____

_____

_____

_____

_____

HOW DID I RESPOND? _____

_____

_____

_____

_____

DAY: 6

ACCOMPLISHMENTS/WINS:

1

2

3

SELF-CARE:

☐ DID I SLEEP WELL?

☐ DID I GET EXERCISE?

☐ DID I GET FRESH AIR?

☐ DID I MEDITATE?

☐ DID I EAT NOURISHING FOODS?

DAILY GRATITUDE:

1.

2.

3.

4.

5.

SOMETHING THAT MADE ME HAPPY TODAY:

DATE _____

OVERALL MOOD:

(HAPPY) (ENERGETIC) (CALM) (STRESSED) (SAD) (TIRED)

❯ THOUGHT LOG: ❮

WHAT WAS ON MY MIND TODAY? _____
_____
_____
_____

HOW MIGHT I REFRAME THOSE THOUGHTS? _____
_____
_____
_____

❯ TRIGGER TRACKER: ❮

DID SOMETHING TRIGGER MY ANXIETY TODAY? _____
_____
_____
_____

HOW DID I RESPOND? _____
_____
_____
_____

DAY: 7

ACCOMPLISHMENTS/WINS:

1	2	3

SELF-CARE:

☐ DID I SLEEP WELL?

☐ DID I GET EXERCISE?

☐ DID I GET FRESH AIR?

☐ DID I MEDITATE?

☐ DID I EAT NOURISHING FOODS?

DAILY GRATITUDE:

1. _____

2. _____

3. _____

4. _____

5. _____

SOMETHING THAT
MADE ME HAPPY TODAY:

WEEKLY FEAR-SETTING:

WHAT AM I WORRIED ABOUT RIGHT NOW? _____

_____

_____

_____

HOW LIKELY IS IT FOR THIS TO ACTUALLY OCCUR? THINK OF YOUR
PAST EXPERIENCES AND WRITE ANY EXAMPLES HERE. _____

_____

_____

_____

WHAT'S THE WORST-CASE SCENARIO?

% CHANCE OF THAT HAPPENING? _____

WHAT'S THE BEST-CASE SCENARIO?

% CHANCE OF THAT HAPPENING? _____

WHAT'S THE MOST LIKELY SCENARIO?

% CHANCE OF THAT HAPPENING? _____

HAPPY HABIT TRACKER:

HABIT TRACKER:	S	M	T	W	T	F	S
	☐	☐	☐	☐	☐	☐	☐
	☐	☐	☐	☐	☐	☐	☐
	☐	☐	☐	☐	☐	☐	☐
	☐	☐	☐	☐	☐	☐	☐
	☐	☐	☐	☐	☐	☐	☐
	☐	☐	☐	☐	☐	☐	☐
	☐	☐	☐	☐	☐	☐	☐
	☐	☐	☐	☐	☐	☐	☐
	☐	☐	☐	☐	☐	☐	☐
	☐	☐	☐	☐	☐	☐	☐
	☐	☐	☐	☐	☐	☐	☐
	☐	☐	☐	☐	☐	☐	☐
	☐	☐	☐	☐	☐	☐	☐
	☐	☐	☐	☐	☐	☐	☐
	☐	☐	☐	☐	☐	☐	☐
	☐	☐	☐	☐	☐	☐	☐

THERAPY REFLECTIONS:

TOPIC WE DISCUSSED:

HOW I FEEL ABOUT IT:

TAKEAWAYS:

FOR NEXT TIME:

MONTH:_____

MONTHLY CHECK-IN:

HOW I FEEL ABOUT THIS
MONTH OVERALL:

WHAT CHANGED SINCE LAST MONTH?

ACCOMPLISHMENTS:

1	2	3

THINGS I WANT TO IMPROVE OR ACCOMPLISH NEXT MONTH:

MEASURE YOUR SATISFACTION:

VERY UNSATISFIED   INDIFFERENT   VERY SATISFIED

O————————————O————————————O

0   1   2   3   4   5   6

HOUSING SITUATION: _____   ENERGY/MOTIVATION: _____

FAMILY: _____   WORK/LIFE BALANCE: _____

FRIENDS: _____   OVERALL HEALTH: _____

SPOUSE/PARTNER: _____   DOCTOR/THERAPIST: _____

SENSE OF COMMUNITY: _____   MONEY/FINANCES: _____

HOBBIES/ACTIVITIES: _____   LIFE PURPOSE: _____

SCHOOL/WORK: _____   QUALITY OF LIFE: _____

3 AREAS OF MY LIFE WHERE I'D LIKE TO IMPROVE:

1. _____
2. _____
3. _____

3 IDEAS FOR HOW I CAN MAKE PROGRESS:

1. _____
2. _____
3. _____

WEEK 5:

DATE _____

OVERALL MOOD:

(HAPPY) (ENERGETIC) (CALM) (STRESSED) (SAD) (TIRED)

❯ THOUGHT LOG: ❮

WHAT WAS ON MY MIND TODAY? _____

_____

_____

_____

HOW MIGHT I REFRAME THOSE THOUGHTS? _____

_____

_____

_____

❯ TRIGGER TRACKER: ❮

DID SOMETHING TRIGGER MY ANXIETY TODAY? _____

_____

_____

_____

HOW DID I RESPOND? _____

_____

_____

_____

DAY: 1

ACCOMPLISHMENTS/WINS:

1	2	3

SELF-CARE:

☐ DID I SLEEP WELL?

☐ DID I GET EXERCISE?

☐ DID I GET FRESH AIR?

☐ DID I MEDITATE?

☐ DID I EAT NOURISHING
FOODS?

DAILY GRATITUDE:

1. _____

2. _____

3. _____

4. _____

5. _____

SOMETHING THAT
MADE ME HAPPY TODAY:

DATE_____

OVERALL MOOD:

(HAPPY)　(ENERGETIC)　(CALM)　(STRESSED)　(SAD)　(TIRED)

❯ THOUGHT LOG: ❮

WHAT WAS ON MY MIND TODAY? _____

_____

_____

_____

HOW MIGHT I REFRAME THOSE THOUGHTS? _____

_____

_____

_____

❯ TRIGGER TRACKER: ❮

DID SOMETHING TRIGGER MY ANXIETY TODAY? _____

_____

_____

_____

HOW DID I RESPOND? _____

_____

_____

_____

ACCOMPLISHMENTS/WINS:

1	2	3

SELF-CARE:

☐ DID I SLEEP WELL?

☐ DID I GET EXERCISE?

☐ DID I GET FRESH AIR?

☐ DID I MEDITATE?

☐ DID I EAT NOURISHING
  FOODS?

DAILY GRATITUDE:

1. _____

2. _____

3. _____

4. _____

5. _____

SOMETHING THAT
MADE ME HAPPY TODAY:

DATE _____

OVERALL MOOD:

(HAPPY) (ENERGETIC) (CALM) (STRESSED) (SAD) (TIRED)

❯ THOUGHT LOG: ❮

WHAT WAS ON MY MIND TODAY? _____
_____
_____
_____

HOW MIGHT I REFRAME THOSE THOUGHTS? _____
_____
_____
_____

❯ TRIGGER TRACKER: ❮

DID SOMETHING TRIGGER MY ANXIETY TODAY? _____
_____
_____
_____

HOW DID I RESPOND? _____
_____
_____
_____

DAY: 3

ACCOMPLISHMENTS/WINS:

1	2	3

SELF-CARE:

- ☐ DID I SLEEP WELL?
- ☐ DID I GET EXERCISE?
- ☐ DID I GET FRESH AIR?
- ☐ DID I MEDITATE?
- ☐ DID I EAT NOURISHING FOODS?

DAILY GRATITUDE:

1. _____
2. _____
3. _____
4. _____
5. _____

SOMETHING THAT
MADE ME HAPPY TODAY:

DATE _____

OVERALL MOOD:

(HAPPY) (ENERGETIC) (CALM) (STRESSED) (SAD) (TIRED)

❯ THOUGHT LOG: ❮

WHAT WAS ON MY MIND TODAY? _____
_____
_____
_____

HOW MIGHT I REFRAME THOSE THOUGHTS? _____
_____
_____
_____

❯ TRIGGER TRACKER: ❮

DID SOMETHING TRIGGER MY ANXIETY TODAY? _____
_____
_____
_____

HOW DID I RESPOND? _____
_____
_____
_____

ACCOMPLISHMENTS/WINS:

1	2	3

SELF-CARE:

☐ DID I SLEEP WELL?

☐ DID I GET EXERCISE?

☐ DID I GET FRESH AIR?

☐ DID I MEDITATE?

☐ DID I EAT NOURISHING
FOODS?

DAILY GRATITUDE:

1. _____

2. _____

3. _____

4. _____

5. _____

SOMETHING THAT
MADE ME HAPPY TODAY:

DATE_____

OVERALL MOOD:

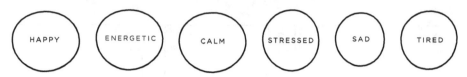

(HAPPY) (ENERGETIC) (CALM) (STRESSED) (SAD) (TIRED)

❯ THOUGHT LOG: ❮

WHAT WAS ON MY MIND TODAY? _____

_____

_____

_____

HOW MIGHT I REFRAME THOSE THOUGHTS? _____

_____

_____

_____

❯ TRIGGER TRACKER: ❮

DID SOMETHING TRIGGER MY ANXIETY TODAY? _____

_____

_____

_____

HOW DID I RESPOND? _____

_____

_____

_____

DAY: 5

ACCOMPLISHMENTS/WINS:

1	2	3

SELF-CARE:

☐ DID I SLEEP WELL?

☐ DID I GET EXERCISE?

☐ DID I GET FRESH AIR?

☐ DID I MEDITATE?

☐ DID I EAT NOURISHING FOODS?

DAILY GRATITUDE:

1. _____

2. _____

3. _____

4. _____

5. _____

SOMETHING THAT
MADE ME HAPPY TODAY:

DATE _____

OVERALL MOOD:

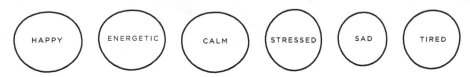

(HAPPY)   (ENERGETIC)   (CALM)   (STRESSED)   (SAD)   (TIRED)

❯ THOUGHT LOG: ❮

WHAT WAS ON MY MIND TODAY? _____

_____

_____

_____

HOW MIGHT I REFRAME THOSE THOUGHTS? _____

_____

_____

_____

❯ TRIGGER TRACKER: ❮

DID SOMETHING TRIGGER MY ANXIETY TODAY? _____

_____

_____

_____

HOW DID I RESPOND? _____

_____

_____

_____

ACCOMPLISHMENTS/WINS:

1	2	3

SELF-CARE:

☐ DID I SLEEP WELL?

☐ DID I GET EXERCISE?

☐ DID I GET FRESH AIR?

☐ DID I MEDITATE?

☐ DID I EAT NOURISHING
FOODS?

DAILY GRATITUDE:

1. _____

2. _____

3. _____

4. _____

5. _____

SOMETHING THAT
MADE ME HAPPY TODAY:

DATE _____

OVERALL MOOD:

(HAPPY) (ENERGETIC) (CALM) (STRESSED) (SAD) (TIRED)

> **THOUGHT LOG:** ◄

WHAT WAS ON MY MIND TODAY? _____
_____
_____
_____

HOW MIGHT I REFRAME THOSE THOUGHTS? _____
_____
_____
_____
_____

> **TRIGGER TRACKER:** ◄

DID SOMETHING TRIGGER MY ANXIETY TODAY? _____
_____
_____
_____

HOW DID I RESPOND? _____
_____
_____
_____

ACCOMPLISHMENTS/WINS:

1	2	3

SELF-CARE:

☐ DID I SLEEP WELL?

☐ DID I GET EXERCISE?

☐ DID I GET FRESH AIR?

☐ DID I MEDITATE?

☐ DID I EAT NOURISHING FOODS?

DAILY GRATITUDE:

1. _____

2. _____

3. _____

4. _____

5. _____

SOMETHING THAT
MADE ME HAPPY TODAY:

WEEKLY ENTRY:

WHAT AM I WORRIED ABOUT RIGHT NOW? _____
_____
_____
_____

HOW LIKELY IS IT FOR THIS TO ACTUALLY OCCUR? THINK OF YOUR
PAST EXPERIENCES AND WRITE ANY EXAMPLES HERE. _____
_____
_____
_____

WHAT'S THE WORST-CASE SCENARIO?

% CHANCE OF THAT HAPPENING? _____

WHAT'S THE BEST-CASE SCENARIO?

% CHANCE OF THAT HAPPENING? _____

WHAT'S THE MOST LIKELY SCENARIO?

% CHANCE OF THAT HAPPENING? _____

HAPPY HABIT TRACKER:

HABIT TRACKER:	S	M	T	W	T	F	S
	□	□	□	□	□	□	□
	□	□	□	□	□	□	□
	□	□	□	□	□	□	□
	□	□	□	□	□	□	□
	□	□	□	□	□	□	□
	□	□	□	□	□	□	□
	□	□	□	□	□	□	□
	□	□	□	□	□	□	□
	□	□	□	□	□	□	□
	□	□	□	□	□	□	□
	□	□	□	□	□	□	□
	□	□	□	□	□	□	□
	□	□	□	□	□	□	□
	□	□	□	□	□	□	□
	□	□	□	□	□	□	□
	□	□	□	□	□	□	□

THERAPY REFLECTIONS:

TOPIC WE DISCUSSED:
....

HOW I FEEL ABOUT IT:
....

TAKEAWAYS:
....

FOR NEXT TIME:
....

WEEK 6:

DATE _____

OVERALL MOOD:

(HAPPY) (ENERGETIC) (CALM) (STRESSED) (SAD) (TIRED)

❯ THOUGHT LOG: ❮

WHAT WAS ON MY MIND TODAY? _____

_____

_____

_____

_____

HOW MIGHT I REFRAME THOSE THOUGHTS? _____

_____

_____

_____

_____

❯ TRIGGER TRACKER: ❮

DID SOMETHING TRIGGER MY ANXIETY TODAY? _____

_____

_____

_____

_____

HOW DID I RESPOND? _____

_____

_____

_____

_____

DAY: 1

ACCOMPLISHMENTS/WINS:

1	2	3

SELF-CARE:

- ☐ DID I SLEEP WELL?
- ☐ DID I GET EXERCISE?
- ☐ DID I GET FRESH AIR?
- ☐ DID I MEDITATE?
- ☐ DID I EAT NOURISHING FOODS?

DAILY GRATITUDE:

1. _____
2. _____
3. _____
4. _____
5. _____

SOMETHING THAT
MADE ME HAPPY TODAY:

DATE_____

OVERALL MOOD:

(HAPPY)　(ENERGETIC)　(CALM)　(STRESSED)　(SAD)　(TIRED)

➤ THOUGHT LOG: ◄

WHAT WAS ON MY MIND TODAY? _____

_____

_____

_____

HOW MIGHT I REFRAME THOSE THOUGHTS? _____

_____

_____

_____

➤ TRIGGER TRACKER: ◄

DID SOMETHING TRIGGER MY ANXIETY TODAY? _____

_____

_____

_____

HOW DID I RESPOND? _____

_____

_____

_____

ACCOMPLISHMENTS/WINS:

1	2	3

SELF-CARE:

☐ DID I SLEEP WELL?

☐ DID I GET EXERCISE?

☐ DID I GET FRESH AIR?

☐ DID I MEDITATE?

☐ DID I EAT NOURISHING FOODS?

DAILY GRATITUDE:

1. _____

2. _____

3. _____

4. _____

5. _____

SOMETHING THAT
MADE ME HAPPY TODAY:

DATE _____

OVERALL MOOD:

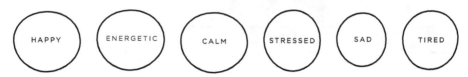

(HAPPY) (ENERGETIC) (CALM) (STRESSED) (SAD) (TIRED)

> **THOUGHT LOG:** ❮

WHAT WAS ON MY MIND TODAY? _____
_____
_____
_____

HOW MIGHT I REFRAME THOSE THOUGHTS? _____
_____
_____
_____

> **TRIGGER TRACKER:** ❮

DID SOMETHING TRIGGER MY ANXIETY TODAY? _____
_____
_____
_____

HOW DID I RESPOND? _____
_____
_____
_____

ACCOMPLISHMENTS/WINS:

1	2	3

SELF-CARE:

☐ DID I SLEEP WELL?

☐ DID I GET EXERCISE?

☐ DID I GET FRESH AIR?

☐ DID I MEDITATE?

☐ DID I EAT NOURISHING FOODS?

DAILY GRATITUDE:

1. _____

2. _____

3. _____

4. _____

5. _____

SOMETHING THAT
MADE ME HAPPY TODAY:

DATE _____

OVERALL MOOD:

(HAPPY)　(ENERGETIC)　(CALM)　(STRESSED)　(SAD)　(TIRED)

❯ THOUGHT LOG: ❮

WHAT WAS ON MY MIND TODAY? _____

_____

_____

_____

HOW MIGHT I REFRAME THOSE THOUGHTS? _____

_____

_____

_____

_____

❯ TRIGGER TRACKER: ❮

DID SOMETHING TRIGGER MY ANXIETY TODAY? _____

_____

_____

_____

HOW DID I RESPOND? _____

_____

_____

_____

_____

ACCOMPLISHMENTS/WINS:

1	2	3

SELF-CARE:

☐ DID I SLEEP WELL?

☐ DID I GET EXERCISE?

☐ DID I GET FRESH AIR?

☐ DID I MEDITATE?

☐ DID I EAT NOURISHING FOODS?

DAILY GRATITUDE:

1. _____

2. _____

3. _____

4. _____

5. _____

SOMETHING THAT MADE ME HAPPY TODAY:

DATE_____

OVERALL MOOD:

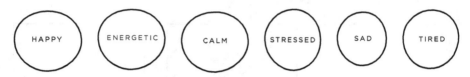

(HAPPY) (ENERGETIC) (CALM) (STRESSED) (SAD) (TIRED)

➤ THOUGHT LOG: ◄

WHAT WAS ON MY MIND TODAY? _____
_____
_____
_____
_____

HOW MIGHT I REFRAME THOSE THOUGHTS? _____
_____
_____
_____
_____

➤ TRIGGER TRACKER: ◄

DID SOMETHING TRIGGER MY ANXIETY TODAY? _____
_____
_____
_____
_____

HOW DID I RESPOND? _____
_____
_____
_____
_____

DAY: 5

ACCOMPLISHMENTS/WINS:

1

2

3

SELF-CARE:

☐ DID I SLEEP WELL?

☐ DID I GET EXERCISE?

☐ DID I GET FRESH AIR?

☐ DID I MEDITATE?

☐ DID I EAT NOURISHING
   FOODS?

DAILY GRATITUDE:

1. _____

2. _____

3. _____

4. _____

5. _____

SOMETHING THAT
MADE ME HAPPY TODAY:

DATE _____

OVERALL MOOD:

(HAPPY) (ENERGETIC) (CALM) (STRESSED) (SAD) (TIRED)

❯ THOUGHT LOG: ❮

WHAT WAS ON MY MIND TODAY? _____

_____

_____

_____

HOW MIGHT I REFRAME THOSE THOUGHTS? _____

_____

_____

_____

❯ TRIGGER TRACKER: ❮

DID SOMETHING TRIGGER MY ANXIETY TODAY? _____

_____

_____

_____

HOW DID I RESPOND? _____

_____

_____

_____

ACCOMPLISHMENTS/WINS:

1	2	3

SELF-CARE:

☐ DID I SLEEP WELL?

☐ DID I GET EXERCISE?

☐ DID I GET FRESH AIR?

☐ DID I MEDITATE?

☐ DID I EAT NOURISHING
    FOODS?

DAILY GRATITUDE:

1. _____

2. _____

3. _____

4. _____

5. _____

SOMETHING THAT
MADE ME HAPPY TODAY:

DATE_____

OVERALL MOOD:

(HAPPY)   (ENERGETIC)   (CALM)   (STRESSED)   (SAD)   (TIRED)

➤ THOUGHT LOG: ❮

WHAT WAS ON MY MIND TODAY? _____

_____

_____

_____

HOW MIGHT I REFRAME THOSE THOUGHTS? _____

_____

_____

_____

_____

➤ TRIGGER TRACKER: ❮

DID SOMETHING TRIGGER MY ANXIETY TODAY? _____

_____

_____

_____

HOW DID I RESPOND? _____

_____

_____

_____

ACCOMPLISHMENTS/WINS:

1	2	3

SELF-CARE:

☐ DID I SLEEP WELL?

☐ DID I GET EXERCISE?

☐ DID I GET FRESH AIR?

☐ DID I MEDITATE?

☐ DID I EAT NOURISHING FOODS?

DAILY GRATITUDE:

1. _____

2. _____

3. _____

4. _____

5. _____

SOMETHING THAT MADE ME HAPPY TODAY:

WEEKLY FEAR-SETTING:

WHAT AM I WORRIED ABOUT RIGHT NOW? _____

_____

_____

_____

HOW LIKELY IS IT FOR THIS TO ACTUALLY OCCUR? THINK OF YOUR
PAST EXPERIENCES AND WRITE ANY EXAMPLES HERE. _____

_____

_____

_____

WHAT'S THE WORST-CASE SCENARIO?

% CHANCE OF THAT HAPPENING? _____

WHAT'S THE BEST-CASE SCENARIO?

% CHANCE OF THAT HAPPENING? _____

WHAT'S THE MOST LIKELY SCENARIO?

% CHANCE OF THAT HAPPENING? _____

HAPPY HABIT TRACKER:

HABIT TRACKER:	S	M	T	W	T	F	S
	☐	☐	☐	☐	☐	☐	☐
	☐	☐	☐	☐	☐	☐	☐
	☐	☐	☐	☐	☐	☐	☐
	☐	☐	☐	☐	☐	☐	☐
	☐	☐	☐	☐	☐	☐	☐
	☐	☐	☐	☐	☐	☐	☐
	☐	☐	☐	☐	☐	☐	☐
	☐	☐	☐	☐	☐	☐	☐
	☐	☐	☐	☐	☐	☐	☐
	☐	☐	☐	☐	☐	☐	☐
	☐	☐	☐	☐	☐	☐	☐
	☐	☐	☐	☐	☐	☐	☐
	☐	☐	☐	☐	☐	☐	☐
	☐	☐	☐	☐	☐	☐	☐
	☐	☐	☐	☐	☐	☐	☐
	☐	☐	☐	☐	☐	☐	☐

THERAPY REFLECTIONS:

TOPIC WE DISCUSSED:	**HOW I FEEL ABOUT IT:**
TAKEAWAYS:	**FOR NEXT TIME:**

WEEK 7:

DATE _____

OVERALL MOOD:

(HAPPY) (ENERGETIC) (CALM) (STRESSED) (SAD) (TIRED)

❯ THOUGHT LOG: ❮

WHAT WAS ON MY MIND TODAY? _____

_____

_____

_____

HOW MIGHT I REFRAME THOSE THOUGHTS? _____

_____

_____

_____

❯ TRIGGER TRACKER: ❮

DID SOMETHING TRIGGER MY ANXIETY TODAY? _____

_____

_____

_____

HOW DID I RESPOND? _____

_____

_____

_____

ACCOMPLISHMENTS/WINS:

1	2	3

SELF-CARE:

☐ DID I SLEEP WELL?

☐ DID I GET EXERCISE?

☐ DID I GET FRESH AIR?

☐ DID I MEDITATE?

☐ DID I EAT NOURISHING
　FOODS?

DAILY GRATITUDE:

1. _____

2. _____

3. _____

4. _____

5. _____

SOMETHING THAT
MADE ME HAPPY TODAY:

DATE _____

OVERALL MOOD:

HAPPY   ENERGETIC   CALM   STRESSED   SAD   TIRED

➤ THOUGHT LOG: ◀

WHAT WAS ON MY MIND TODAY? _____

_____

_____

_____

HOW MIGHT I REFRAME THOSE THOUGHTS? _____

_____

_____

_____

➤ TRIGGER TRACKER: ◀

DID SOMETHING TRIGGER MY ANXIETY TODAY? _____

_____

_____

_____

HOW DID I RESPOND? _____

_____

_____

_____

DAY: 2

ACCOMPLISHMENTS/WINS:

1

2

3

SELF-CARE:

☐ DID I SLEEP WELL?

☐ DID I GET EXERCISE?

☐ DID I GET FRESH AIR?

☐ DID I MEDITATE?

☐ DID I EAT NOURISHING
   FOODS?

DAILY GRATITUDE:

1. _____

2. _____

3. _____

4. _____

5. _____

SOMETHING THAT
MADE ME HAPPY TODAY:

DATE _____

OVERALL MOOD:

(HAPPY)   (ENERGETIC)   (CALM)   (STRESSED)   (SAD)   (TIRED)

➤ THOUGHT LOG: ◄

WHAT WAS ON MY MIND TODAY? _____

_____

_____

_____

HOW MIGHT I REFRAME THOSE THOUGHTS? _____

_____

_____

_____

➤ TRIGGER TRACKER: ◄

DID SOMETHING TRIGGER MY ANXIETY TODAY? _____

_____

_____

_____

HOW DID I RESPOND? _____

_____

_____

_____

DAY: 3

ACCOMPLISHMENTS/WINS:

1	2	3

SELF-CARE:

☐ DID I SLEEP WELL?

☐ DID I GET EXERCISE?

☐ DID I GET FRESH AIR?

☐ DID I MEDITATE?

☐ DID I EAT NOURISHING FOODS?

DAILY GRATITUDE:

1. _____

2. _____

3. _____

4. _____

5. _____

SOMETHING THAT
MADE ME HAPPY TODAY:

DATE_____

OVERALL MOOD:

(HAPPY) (ENERGETIC) (CALM) (STRESSED) (SAD) (TIRED)

➤ THOUGHT LOG: ◄

WHAT WAS ON MY MIND TODAY? _____

_____

_____

_____

_____

HOW MIGHT I REFRAME THOSE THOUGHTS? _____

_____

_____

_____

_____

➤ TRIGGER TRACKER: ◄

DID SOMETHING TRIGGER MY ANXIETY TODAY? _____

_____

_____

_____

_____

HOW DID I RESPOND? _____

_____

_____

_____

_____

ACCOMPLISHMENTS/WINS:

1	2	3

SELF-CARE:

- ☐ DID I SLEEP WELL?
- ☐ DID I GET EXERCISE?
- ☐ DID I GET FRESH AIR?
- ☐ DID I MEDITATE?
- ☐ DID I EAT NOURISHING FOODS?

DAILY GRATITUDE:

1. _____
2. _____
3. _____
4. _____
5. _____

**SOMETHING THAT
MADE ME HAPPY TODAY:**

DATE _____

OVERALL MOOD:

(HAPPY) (ENERGETIC) (CALM) (STRESSED) (SAD) (TIRED)

❯ THOUGHT LOG: ❮

WHAT WAS ON MY MIND TODAY? _____

_____

_____

_____

HOW MIGHT I REFRAME THOSE THOUGHTS? _____

_____

_____

_____

❯ TRIGGER TRACKER: ❮

DID SOMETHING TRIGGER MY ANXIETY TODAY? _____

_____

_____

_____

HOW DID I RESPOND? _____

_____

_____

_____

DAY: 5

ACCOMPLISHMENTS/WINS:

1

2

3

SELF-CARE:

☐ DID I SLEEP WELL?

☐ DID I GET EXERCISE?

☐ DID I GET FRESH AIR?

☐ DID I MEDITATE?

☐ DID I EAT NOURISHING
FOODS?

DAILY GRATITUDE:

1. _____

2. _____

3. _____

4. _____

5. _____

SOMETHING THAT
MADE ME HAPPY TODAY:

DATE _____

OVERALL MOOD:

(HAPPY) (ENERGETIC) (CALM) (STRESSED) (SAD) (TIRED)

> **THOUGHT LOG:** ❮

WHAT WAS ON MY MIND TODAY? _____
_____
_____
_____

HOW MIGHT I REFRAME THOSE THOUGHTS? _____
_____
_____
_____

> **TRIGGER TRACKER:** ❮

DID SOMETHING TRIGGER MY ANXIETY TODAY? _____
_____
_____
_____

HOW DID I RESPOND? _____
_____
_____
_____

DAY: 6

ACCOMPLISHMENTS/WINS:

1	2	3

SELF-CARE:

- ☐ DID I SLEEP WELL?
- ☐ DID I GET EXERCISE?
- ☐ DID I GET FRESH AIR?
- ☐ DID I MEDITATE?
- ☐ DID I EAT NOURISHING FOODS?

DAILY GRATITUDE:

1. _____
2. _____
3. _____
4. _____
5. _____

SOMETHING THAT
MADE ME HAPPY TODAY:

DATE _____

OVERALL MOOD:

(HAPPY) (ENERGETIC) (CALM) (STRESSED) (SAD) (TIRED)

> **THOUGHT LOG:** ❮

WHAT WAS ON MY MIND TODAY? _____

_____

_____

_____

_____

HOW MIGHT I REFRAME THOSE THOUGHTS? _____

_____

_____

_____

_____

> **TRIGGER TRACKER:** ❮

DID SOMETHING TRIGGER MY ANXIETY TODAY? _____

_____

_____

_____

_____

HOW DID I RESPOND? _____

_____

_____

_____

_____

ACCOMPLISHMENTS/WINS:

1	2	3

SELF-CARE:

☐ DID I SLEEP WELL?

☐ DID I GET EXERCISE?

☐ DID I GET FRESH AIR?

☐ DID I MEDITATE?

☐ DID I EAT NOURISHING FOODS?

DAILY GRATITUDE:

1. _____

2. _____

3. _____

4. _____

5. _____

SOMETHING THAT MADE ME HAPPY TODAY:

WEEKLY FEAR-SETTING:

WHAT AM I WORRIED ABOUT RIGHT NOW? _____

_____

_____

_____

HOW LIKELY IS IT FOR THIS TO ACTUALLY OCCUR? THINK OF YOUR
PAST EXPERIENCES AND WRITE ANY EXAMPLES HERE. _____

_____

_____

_____

WHAT'S THE WORST-CASE SCENARIO?

% CHANCE OF THAT HAPPENING? _____

WHAT'S THE BEST-CASE SCENARIO?

% CHANCE OF THAT HAPPENING? _____

WHAT'S THE MOST LIKELY SCENARIO?

% CHANCE OF THAT HAPPENING? _____

HAPPY HABIT TRACKER:

HABIT TRACKER:	S	M	T	W	T	F	S
	☐	☐	☐	☐	☐	☐	☐
	☐	☐	☐	☐	☐	☐	☐
	☐	☐	☐	☐	☐	☐	☐
	☐	☐	☐	☐	☐	☐	☐
	☐	☐	☐	☐	☐	☐	☐
	☐	☐	☐	☐	☐	☐	☐
	☐	☐	☐	☐	☐	☐	☐
	☐	☐	☐	☐	☐	☐	☐
	☐	☐	☐	☐	☐	☐	☐
	☐	☐	☐	☐	☐	☐	☐
	☐	☐	☐	☐	☐	☐	☐
	☐	☐	☐	☐	☐	☐	☐
	☐	☐	☐	☐	☐	☐	☐
	☐	☐	☐	☐	☐	☐	☐
	☐	☐	☐	☐	☐	☐	☐
	☐	☐	☐	☐	☐	☐	☐

THERAPY REFLECTIONS:

TOPIC WE DISCUSSED:
....

HOW I FEEL ABOUT IT:
....

TAKEAWAYS:
....

FOR NEXT TIME:
....

WEEK 8:

DATE _____

OVERALL MOOD:

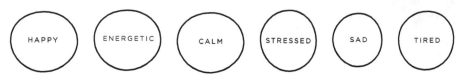

(HAPPY) (ENERGETIC) (CALM) (STRESSED) (SAD) (TIRED)

> **THOUGHT LOG:** <

WHAT WAS ON MY MIND TODAY? _____
_____
_____
_____

HOW MIGHT I REFRAME THOSE THOUGHTS? _____
_____
_____
_____

> **TRIGGER TRACKER:** <

DID SOMETHING TRIGGER MY ANXIETY TODAY? _____
_____
_____
_____

HOW DID I RESPOND? _____
_____
_____
_____

ACCOMPLISHMENTS/WINS:

1

2

3

SELF-CARE:

☐ DID I SLEEP WELL?

☐ DID I GET EXERCISE?

☐ DID I GET FRESH AIR?

☐ DID I MEDITATE?

☐ DID I EAT NOURISHING FOODS?

DAILY GRATITUDE:

1. _____

2. _____

3. _____

4. _____

5. _____

SOMETHING THAT
MADE ME HAPPY TODAY:

DATE _____

OVERALL MOOD:

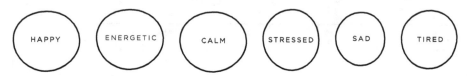

(HAPPY) (ENERGETIC) (CALM) (STRESSED) (SAD) (TIRED)

❯ THOUGHT LOG: ❮

WHAT WAS ON MY MIND TODAY? _____

_____

_____

_____

_____

HOW MIGHT I REFRAME THOSE THOUGHTS? _____

_____

_____

_____

_____

❯ TRIGGER TRACKER: ❮

DID SOMETHING TRIGGER MY ANXIETY TODAY? _____

_____

_____

_____

_____

HOW DID I RESPOND? _____

_____

_____

_____

_____

ACCOMPLISHMENTS/WINS:

1	2	3

SELF-CARE:

☐ DID I SLEEP WELL?

☐ DID I GET EXERCISE?

☐ DID I GET FRESH AIR?

☐ DID I MEDITATE?

☐ DID I EAT NOURISHING FOODS?

DAILY GRATITUDE:

1. _____

2. _____

3. _____

4. _____

5. _____

SOMETHING THAT
MADE ME HAPPY TODAY:

DATE _____

OVERALL MOOD:

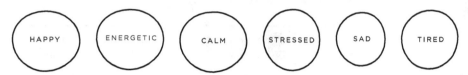

(HAPPY) (ENERGETIC) (CALM) (STRESSED) (SAD) (TIRED)

❯ THOUGHT LOG: ❮

WHAT WAS ON MY MIND TODAY? _____

_____

_____

_____

_____

HOW MIGHT I REFRAME THOSE THOUGHTS? _____

_____

_____

_____

_____

❯ TRIGGER TRACKER: ❮

DID SOMETHING TRIGGER MY ANXIETY TODAY? _____

_____

_____

_____

_____

HOW DID I RESPOND? _____

_____

_____

_____

_____

ACCOMPLISHMENTS/WINS:

1	2	3

SELF-CARE:

☐ DID I SLEEP WELL?

☐ DID I GET EXERCISE?

☐ DID I GET FRESH AIR?

☐ DID I MEDITATE?

☐ DID I EAT NOURISHING
  FOODS?

DAILY GRATITUDE:

1. _____

2. _____

3. _____

4. _____

5. _____

SOMETHING THAT
MADE ME HAPPY TODAY:

DATE _____

OVERALL MOOD:

(HAPPY) (ENERGETIC) (CALM) (STRESSED) (SAD) (TIRED)

❯ THOUGHT LOG: ❮

WHAT WAS ON MY MIND TODAY? _____

_____

_____

_____

HOW MIGHT I REFRAME THOSE THOUGHTS? _____

_____

_____

_____

❯ TRIGGER TRACKER: ❮

DID SOMETHING TRIGGER MY ANXIETY TODAY? _____

_____

_____

_____

HOW DID I RESPOND? _____

_____

_____

_____

DAY: 4

ACCOMPLISHMENTS/WINS:

1	2	3

SELF-CARE:

- ☐ DID I SLEEP WELL?
- ☐ DID I GET EXERCISE?
- ☐ DID I GET FRESH AIR?
- ☐ DID I MEDITATE?
- ☐ DID I EAT NOURISHING FOODS?

DAILY GRATITUDE:

1. _____
2. _____
3. _____
4. _____
5. _____

SOMETHING THAT
MADE ME HAPPY TODAY:

DATE _____

OVERALL MOOD:

(HAPPY)   (ENERGETIC)   (CALM)   (STRESSED)   (SAD)   (TIRED)

❯ THOUGHT LOG: ❮

WHAT WAS ON MY MIND TODAY? _____
_____
_____
_____

HOW MIGHT I REFRAME THOSE THOUGHTS? _____
_____
_____
_____

❯ TRIGGER TRACKER: ❮

DID SOMETHING TRIGGER MY ANXIETY TODAY? _____
_____
_____
_____

HOW DID I RESPOND? _____
_____
_____
_____

DAY: 5

ACCOMPLISHMENTS/WINS:

1	2	3

SELF-CARE:

☐ DID I SLEEP WELL?

☐ DID I GET EXERCISE?

☐ DID I GET FRESH AIR?

☐ DID I MEDITATE?

☐ DID I EAT NOURISHING FOODS?

DAILY GRATITUDE:

1. _____

2. _____

3. _____

4. _____

5. _____

SOMETHING THAT MADE ME HAPPY TODAY:

DATE _____

OVERALL MOOD:

(HAPPY)   (ENERGETIC)   (CALM)   (STRESSED)   (SAD)   (TIRED)

➤ THOUGHT LOG: ◀

WHAT WAS ON MY MIND TODAY? _____

_____

_____

_____

HOW MIGHT I REFRAME THOSE THOUGHTS? _____

_____

_____

_____

➤ TRIGGER TRACKER: ◀

DID SOMETHING TRIGGER MY ANXIETY TODAY? _____

_____

_____

_____

HOW DID I RESPOND? _____

_____

_____

_____

DAY: 6

ACCOMPLISHMENTS/WINS:

1	2	3

SELF-CARE:

☐ DID I SLEEP WELL?

☐ DID I GET EXERCISE?

☐ DID I GET FRESH AIR?

☐ DID I MEDITATE?

☐ DID I EAT NOURISHING
  FOODS?

DAILY GRATITUDE:

1. _____

2. _____

3. _____

4. _____

5. _____

SOMETHING THAT
MADE ME HAPPY TODAY:

DATE _____

OVERALL MOOD:

(HAPPY) (ENERGETIC) (CALM) (STRESSED) (SAD) (TIRED)

➤ THOUGHT LOG: ◄

WHAT WAS ON MY MIND TODAY? _____
_____
_____
_____

HOW MIGHT I REFRAME THOSE THOUGHTS? _____
_____
_____
_____

➤ TRIGGER TRACKER: ◄

DID SOMETHING TRIGGER MY ANXIETY TODAY? _____
_____
_____
_____

HOW DID I RESPOND? _____
_____
_____
_____

DAY: 7

ACCOMPLISHMENTS/WINS:

1	2	3

SELF-CARE:

☐ DID I SLEEP WELL?

☐ DID I GET EXERCISE?

☐ DID I GET FRESH AIR?

☐ DID I MEDITATE?

☐ DID I EAT NOURISHING FOODS?

DAILY GRATITUDE:

1. _____
2. _____
3. _____
4. _____
5. _____

SOMETHING THAT MADE ME HAPPY TODAY:

WEEKLY FEAR-SETTING:

WHAT AM I WORRIED ABOUT RIGHT NOW? _____

_____

_____

_____

HOW LIKELY IS IT FOR THIS TO ACTUALLY OCCUR? THINK OF YOUR
PAST EXPERIENCES AND WRITE ANY EXAMPLES HERE. _____

_____

_____

_____

WHAT'S THE WORST-CASE SCENARIO?

% CHANCE OF THAT HAPPENING? _____

WHAT'S THE BEST-CASE SCENARIO?

% CHANCE OF THAT HAPPENING? _____

WHAT'S THE MOST LIKELY SCENARIO?

% CHANCE OF THAT HAPPENING? _____

HAPPY HABIT TRACKER:

HABIT TRACKER:	S	M	T	W	T	F	S
	☐	☐	☐	☐	☐	☐	☐
	☐	☐	☐	☐	☐	☐	☐
	☐	☐	☐	☐	☐	☐	☐
	☐	☐	☐	☐	☐	☐	☐
	☐	☐	☐	☐	☐	☐	☐
	☐	☐	☐	☐	☐	☐	☐
	☐	☐	☐	☐	☐	☐	☐
	☐	☐	☐	☐	☐	☐	☐
	☐	☐	☐	☐	☐	☐	☐
	☐	☐	☐	☐	☐	☐	☐
	☐	☐	☐	☐	☐	☐	☐
	☐	☐	☐	☐	☐	☐	☐
	☐	☐	☐	☐	☐	☐	☐
	☐	☐	☐	☐	☐	☐	☐
	☐	☐	☐	☐	☐	☐	☐
	☐	☐	☐	☐	☐	☐	☐

THERAPY REFLECTIONS:

TOPIC WE DISCUSSED:
....

HOW I FEEL ABOUT IT:
....

TAKEAWAYS:
....

FOR NEXT TIME:
....

MONTH:_____

MONTHLY CHECK-IN:

HOW I FEEL ABOUT THIS MONTH OVERALL:

WHAT CHANGED SINCE LAST MONTH? _____

_____

_____

_____

ACCOMPLISHMENTS:

1	2	3

THINGS I WANT TO IMPROVE OR ACCOMPLISH NEXT MONTH: _____

_____

_____

_____

_____

MEASURE YOUR SATISFACTION:

VERY UNSATISFIED   INDIFFERENT   VERY SATISFIED

O————————O————————O

0   1   2   3   4   5   6

HOUSING SITUATION: _____   ENERGY/MOTIVATION: _____

FAMILY: _____   WORK/LIFE BALANCE: _____

FRIENDS: _____   OVERALL HEALTH: _____

SPOUSE/PARTNER: _____   DOCTOR/THERAPIST: _____

SENSE OF COMMUNITY: _____   MONEY/FINANCES: _____

HOBBIES/ACTIVITIES: _____   LIFE PURPOSE: _____

SCHOOL/WORK: _____   QUALITY OF LIFE: _____

3 AREAS OF MY LIFE WHERE I'D LIKE TO IMPROVE:

1. _____

2. _____

3. _____

3 IDEAS FOR HOW I CAN MAKE PROGRESS:

1. _____

2. _____

3. _____

WEEK 9:

DATE _____

OVERALL MOOD:

HAPPY   ENERGETIC   CALM   STRESSED   SAD   TIRED

➤ THOUGHT LOG: ❰

WHAT WAS ON MY MIND TODAY? _____

_____

_____

_____

HOW MIGHT I REFRAME THOSE THOUGHTS? _____

_____

_____

_____

➤ TRIGGER TRACKER: ❰

DID SOMETHING TRIGGER MY ANXIETY TODAY? _____

_____

_____

_____

HOW DID I RESPOND? _____

_____

_____

_____

DAY: 1

ACCOMPLISHMENTS/WINS:

1	2	3

SELF-CARE:

☐ DID I SLEEP WELL?

☐ DID I GET EXERCISE?

☐ DID I GET FRESH AIR?

☐ DID I MEDITATE?

☐ DID I EAT NOURISHING
FOODS?

DAILY GRATITUDE:

1. _____

2. _____

3. _____

4. _____

5. _____

SOMETHING THAT
MADE ME HAPPY TODAY:

DATE _____

OVERALL MOOD:

(HAPPY)　(ENERGETIC)　(CALM)　(STRESSED)　(SAD)　(TIRED)

➤ THOUGHT LOG: ◀

WHAT WAS ON MY MIND TODAY? _____
_____
_____
_____

HOW MIGHT I REFRAME THOSE THOUGHTS? _____
_____
_____
_____

➤ TRIGGER TRACKER: ◀

DID SOMETHING TRIGGER MY ANXIETY TODAY? _____
_____
_____
_____

HOW DID I RESPOND? _____
_____
_____
_____

ACCOMPLISHMENTS/WINS:

1	2	3

SELF-CARE:

- ☐ DID I SLEEP WELL?
- ☐ DID I GET EXERCISE?
- ☐ DID I GET FRESH AIR?
- ☐ DID I MEDITATE?
- ☐ DID I EAT NOURISHING FOODS?

DAILY GRATITUDE:

1. _____
2. _____
3. _____
4. _____
5. _____

SOMETHING THAT
MADE ME HAPPY TODAY:

DATE _____

OVERALL MOOD:

(HAPPY) (ENERGETIC) (CALM) (STRESSED) (SAD) (TIRED)

❯ THOUGHT LOG: ❮

WHAT WAS ON MY MIND TODAY? _____
_____
_____
_____

HOW MIGHT I REFRAME THOSE THOUGHTS? _____
_____
_____
_____

❯ TRIGGER TRACKER: ❮

DID SOMETHING TRIGGER MY ANXIETY TODAY? _____
_____
_____
_____

HOW DID I RESPOND? _____
_____
_____
_____

ACCOMPLISHMENTS/WINS:

1	2	3

SELF-CARE:

☐ DID I SLEEP WELL?

☐ DID I GET EXERCISE?

☐ DID I GET FRESH AIR?

☐ DID I MEDITATE?

☐ DID I EAT NOURISHING FOODS?

DAILY GRATITUDE:

1. _____

2. _____

3. _____

4. _____

5. _____

SOMETHING THAT
MADE ME HAPPY TODAY:

DATE _____

OVERALL MOOD:

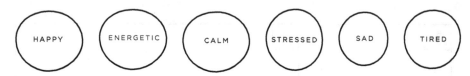

(HAPPY) (ENERGETIC) (CALM) (STRESSED) (SAD) (TIRED)

❯ THOUGHT LOG: ❮

WHAT WAS ON MY MIND TODAY? _____

_____

_____

_____

HOW MIGHT I REFRAME THOSE THOUGHTS? _____

_____

_____

_____

❯ TRIGGER TRACKER: ❮

DID SOMETHING TRIGGER MY ANXIETY TODAY? _____

_____

_____

_____

HOW DID I RESPOND? _____

_____

_____

_____

DAY: 4

ACCOMPLISHMENTS/WINS:

1	2	3

SELF-CARE:

- ☐ DID I SLEEP WELL?
- ☐ DID I GET EXERCISE?
- ☐ DID I GET FRESH AIR?
- ☐ DID I MEDITATE?
- ☐ DID I EAT NOURISHING FOODS?

DAILY GRATITUDE:

1. _____
2. _____
3. _____
4. _____
5. _____

SOMETHING THAT
MADE ME HAPPY TODAY:

DATE _____

OVERALL MOOD:

(HAPPY)   (ENERGETIC)   (CALM)   (STRESSED)   (SAD)   (TIRED)

❯ THOUGHT LOG: ❮

WHAT WAS ON MY MIND TODAY? _____

_____

_____

_____

HOW MIGHT I REFRAME THOSE THOUGHTS? _____

_____

_____

_____

❯ TRIGGER TRACKER: ❮

DID SOMETHING TRIGGER MY ANXIETY TODAY? _____

_____

_____

_____

HOW DID I RESPOND? _____

_____

_____

_____

ACCOMPLISHMENTS/WINS:

1	2	3

SELF-CARE:

☐ DID I SLEEP WELL?

☐ DID I GET EXERCISE?

☐ DID I GET FRESH AIR?

☐ DID I MEDITATE?

☐ DID I EAT NOURISHING FOODS?

DAILY GRATITUDE:

1. _____

2. _____

3. _____

4. _____

5. _____

SOMETHING THAT
MADE ME HAPPY TODAY:

DATE _____

OVERALL MOOD:

(HAPPY)   (ENERGETIC)   (CALM)   (STRESSED)   (SAD)   (TIRED)

➤ THOUGHT LOG: ❰

WHAT WAS ON MY MIND TODAY? _____
_____
_____
_____

HOW MIGHT I REFRAME THOSE THOUGHTS? _____
_____
_____
_____

➤ TRIGGER TRACKER: ❰

DID SOMETHING TRIGGER MY ANXIETY TODAY? _____
_____
_____
_____

HOW DID I RESPOND? _____
_____
_____
_____

ACCOMPLISHMENTS/WINS:

1	2	3

SELF-CARE:

☐ DID I SLEEP WELL?

☐ DID I GET EXERCISE?

☐ DID I GET FRESH AIR?

☐ DID I MEDITATE?

☐ DID I EAT NOURISHING
FOODS?

DAILY GRATITUDE:

1. _____

2. _____

3. _____

4. _____

5. _____

SOMETHING THAT
MADE ME HAPPY TODAY:

DATE _____

OVERALL MOOD:

(HAPPY)   (ENERGETIC)   (CALM)   (STRESSED)   (SAD)   (TIRED)

❯ THOUGHT LOG: ❮

WHAT WAS ON MY MIND TODAY? _____
_____
_____
_____
_____

HOW MIGHT I REFRAME THOSE THOUGHTS? _____
_____
_____
_____
_____

❯ TRIGGER TRACKER: ❮

DID SOMETHING TRIGGER MY ANXIETY TODAY? _____
_____
_____
_____
_____

HOW DID I RESPOND? _____
_____
_____
_____
_____

DAY: 7

ACCOMPLISHMENTS/WINS:

1	2	3

SELF-CARE:

- ☐ DID I SLEEP WELL?
- ☐ DID I GET EXERCISE?
- ☐ DID I GET FRESH AIR?
- ☐ DID I MEDITATE?
- ☐ DID I EAT NOURISHING FOODS?

DAILY GRATITUDE:

1. _____
2. _____
3. _____
4. _____
5. _____

SOMETHING THAT MADE ME HAPPY TODAY:

WEEKLY FEAR-SETTING:

WHAT AM I WORRIED ABOUT RIGHT NOW? _____

_____

_____

_____

HOW LIKELY IS IT FOR THIS TO ACTUALLY OCCUR? THINK OF YOUR
PAST EXPERIENCES AND WRITE ANY EXAMPLES HERE. _____

_____

_____

_____

WHAT'S THE WORST-CASE SCENARIO?

% CHANCE OF THAT HAPPENING? _____

WHAT'S THE BEST-CASE SCENARIO?

% CHANCE OF THAT HAPPENING? _____

WHAT'S THE MOST LIKELY SCENARIO?

% CHANCE OF THAT HAPPENING? _____

HAPPY HABIT TRACKER:

HABIT TRACKER:	S	M	T	W	T	F	S
	□	□	□	□	□	□	□
	□	□	□	□	□	□	□
	□	□	□	□	□	□	□
	□	□	□	□	□	□	□
	□	□	□	□	□	□	□
	□	□	□	□	□	□	□
	□	□	□	□	□	□	□
	□	□	□	□	□	□	□
	□	□	□	□	□	□	□
	□	□	□	□	□	□	□
	□	□	□	□	□	□	□
	□	□	□	□	□	□	□
	□	□	□	□	□	□	□
	□	□	□	□	□	□	□
	□	□	□	□	□	□	□
	□	□	□	□	□	□	□

THERAPY REFLECTIONS:

TOPIC WE DISCUSSED:
....

HOW I FEEL ABOUT IT:
....

TAKEAWAYS:
....

FOR NEXT TIME:
....

WEEK 10:

DATE _____

OVERALL MOOD:

(HAPPY)   (ENERGETIC)   (CALM)   (STRESSED)   (SAD)   (TIRED)

➤ THOUGHT LOG: ◄

WHAT WAS ON MY MIND TODAY? _____

_____

_____

_____

HOW MIGHT I REFRAME THOSE THOUGHTS? _____

_____

_____

_____

➤ TRIGGER TRACKER: ◄

DID SOMETHING TRIGGER MY ANXIETY TODAY? _____

_____

_____

_____

HOW DID I RESPOND? _____

_____

_____

_____

ACCOMPLISHMENTS/WINS:

1	2	3

SELF-CARE:

- ☐ DID I SLEEP WELL?
- ☐ DID I GET EXERCISE?
- ☐ DID I GET FRESH AIR?
- ☐ DID I MEDITATE?
- ☐ DID I EAT NOURISHING FOODS?

DAILY GRATITUDE:

1. _____
2. _____
3. _____
4. _____
5. _____

SOMETHING THAT
MADE ME HAPPY TODAY:

DATE _____

OVERALL MOOD:

HAPPY   ENERGETIC   CALM   STRESSED   SAD   TIRED

❯ THOUGHT LOG: ❮

WHAT WAS ON MY MIND TODAY? _____

_____

_____

_____

HOW MIGHT I REFRAME THOSE THOUGHTS? _____

_____

_____

_____

❯ TRIGGER TRACKER: ❮

DID SOMETHING TRIGGER MY ANXIETY TODAY? _____

_____

_____

_____

HOW DID I RESPOND? _____

_____

_____

_____

ACCOMPLISHMENTS/WINS:

1	2	3

SELF-CARE:

☐ DID I SLEEP WELL?

☐ DID I GET EXERCISE?

☐ DID I GET FRESH AIR?

☐ DID I MEDITATE?

☐ DID I EAT NOURISHING FOODS?

DAILY GRATITUDE:

1. _____

2. _____

3. _____

4. _____

5. _____

SOMETHING THAT
MADE ME HAPPY TODAY:

DATE _____

OVERALL MOOD:

(HAPPY) (ENERGETIC) (CALM) (STRESSED) (SAD) (TIRED)

❯ THOUGHT LOG: ❮

WHAT WAS ON MY MIND TODAY? _____

_____

_____

_____

HOW MIGHT I REFRAME THOSE THOUGHTS? _____

_____

_____

_____

❯ TRIGGER TRACKER: ❮

DID SOMETHING TRIGGER MY ANXIETY TODAY? _____

_____

_____

_____

HOW DID I RESPOND? _____

_____

_____

_____

DAY: 3

ACCOMPLISHMENTS/WINS:

1

2

3

SELF-CARE:

☐ DID I SLEEP WELL?

☐ DID I GET EXERCISE?

☐ DID I GET FRESH AIR?

☐ DID I MEDITATE?

☐ DID I EAT NOURISHING FOODS?

DAILY GRATITUDE:

1. _____

2. _____

3. _____

4. _____

5. _____

SOMETHING THAT
MADE ME HAPPY TODAY:

DATE_____

OVERALL MOOD:

(HAPPY)   (ENERGETIC)   (CALM)   (STRESSED)   (SAD)   (TIRED)

❯ THOUGHT LOG: ❮

WHAT WAS ON MY MIND TODAY? _____

_____

_____

_____

HOW MIGHT I REFRAME THOSE THOUGHTS? _____

_____

_____

_____

❯ TRIGGER TRACKER: ❮

DID SOMETHING TRIGGER MY ANXIETY TODAY? _____

_____

_____

_____

HOW DID I RESPOND? _____

_____

_____

_____

DAY: 4

ACCOMPLISHMENTS/WINS:

1	2	3

SELF-CARE:

☐ DID I SLEEP WELL?

☐ DID I GET EXERCISE?

☐ DID I GET FRESH AIR?

☐ DID I MEDITATE?

☐ DID I EAT NOURISHING FOODS?

DAILY GRATITUDE:

1. _____

2. _____

3. _____

4. _____

5. _____

SOMETHING THAT
MADE ME HAPPY TODAY:

DATE _____

OVERALL MOOD:

(HAPPY) (ENERGETIC) (CALM) (STRESSED) (SAD) (TIRED)

❯ THOUGHT LOG: ❮

WHAT WAS ON MY MIND TODAY? _____

_____

_____

_____

HOW MIGHT I REFRAME THOSE THOUGHTS? _____

_____

_____

_____

_____

❯ TRIGGER TRACKER: ❮

DID SOMETHING TRIGGER MY ANXIETY TODAY? _____

_____

_____

_____

HOW DID I RESPOND? _____

_____

_____

_____

_____

ACCOMPLISHMENTS/WINS:

1	2	3

SELF-CARE:

☐ DID I SLEEP WELL?

☐ DID I GET EXERCISE?

☐ DID I GET FRESH AIR?

☐ DID I MEDITATE?

☐ DID I EAT NOURISHING FOODS?

DAILY GRATITUDE:

1. _____

2. _____

3. _____

4. _____

5. _____

SOMETHING THAT
MADE ME HAPPY TODAY:

DATE _____

OVERALL MOOD:

(HAPPY)   (ENERGETIC)   (CALM)   (STRESSED)   (SAD)   (TIRED)

➤ THOUGHT LOG: ◄

WHAT WAS ON MY MIND TODAY? _____

_____

_____

_____

HOW MIGHT I REFRAME THOSE THOUGHTS? _____

_____

_____

_____

➤ TRIGGER TRACKER: ◄

DID SOMETHING TRIGGER MY ANXIETY TODAY? _____

_____

_____

_____

HOW DID I RESPOND? _____

_____

_____

_____

DAY: 6

ACCOMPLISHMENTS/WINS:

1

2

3

SELF-CARE:

☐ DID I SLEEP WELL?

☐ DID I GET EXERCISE?

☐ DID I GET FRESH AIR?

☐ DID I MEDITATE?

☐ DID I EAT NOURISHING FOODS?

DAILY GRATITUDE:

1. _____

2. _____

3. _____

4. _____

5. _____

SOMETHING THAT
MADE ME HAPPY TODAY:

DATE _____

OVERALL MOOD:

HAPPY   ENERGETIC   CALM   STRESSED   SAD   TIRED

❯ THOUGHT LOG: ❮

WHAT WAS ON MY MIND TODAY? _____
_____
_____
_____

HOW MIGHT I REFRAME THOSE THOUGHTS? _____
_____
_____
_____

❯ TRIGGER TRACKER: ❮

DID SOMETHING TRIGGER MY ANXIETY TODAY? _____
_____
_____
_____

HOW DID I RESPOND? _____
_____
_____
_____

ACCOMPLISHMENTS/WINS:

1	2	3

SELF-CARE:

- ☐ DID I SLEEP WELL?
- ☐ DID I GET EXERCISE?
- ☐ DID I GET FRESH AIR?
- ☐ DID I MEDITATE?
- ☐ DID I EAT NOURISHING FOODS?

DAILY GRATITUDE:

1. _____
2. _____
3. _____
4. _____
5. _____

**SOMETHING THAT
MADE ME HAPPY TODAY:**

WEEKLY FEAR-SETTING:

WHAT AM I WORRIED ABOUT RIGHT NOW? _____

_____

_____

_____

HOW LIKELY IS IT FOR THIS TO ACTUALLY OCCUR? THINK OF YOUR
PAST EXPERIENCES AND WRITE ANY EXAMPLES HERE. _____

_____

_____

_____

WHAT'S THE WORST-CASE SCENARIO?

% CHANCE OF THAT HAPPENING? _____

WHAT'S THE BEST-CASE SCENARIO?

% CHANCE OF THAT HAPPENING? _____

WHAT'S THE MOST LIKELY SCENARIO?

% CHANCE OF THAT HAPPENING? _____

HAPPY HABIT TRACKER:

HABIT TRACKER:	S	M	T	W	T	F	S
	☐	☐	☐	☐	☐	☐	☐
	☐	☐	☐	☐	☐	☐	☐
	☐	☐	☐	☐	☐	☐	☐
	☐	☐	☐	☐	☐	☐	☐
	☐	☐	☐	☐	☐	☐	☐
	☐	☐	☐	☐	☐	☐	☐
	☐	☐	☐	☐	☐	☐	☐
	☐	☐	☐	☐	☐	☐	☐
	☐	☐	☐	☐	☐	☐	☐
	☐	☐	☐	☐	☐	☐	☐
	☐	☐	☐	☐	☐	☐	☐
	☐	☐	☐	☐	☐	☐	☐
	☐	☐	☐	☐	☐	☐	☐
	☐	☐	☐	☐	☐	☐	☐
	☐	☐	☐	☐	☐	☐	☐
	☐	☐	☐	☐	☐	☐	☐

THERAPY REFLECTIONS:

TOPIC WE DISCUSSED:
....

HOW I FEEL ABOUT IT:
....

TAKEAWAYS:
....

FOR NEXT TIME:
....

WEEK 11:

DATE _____

OVERALL MOOD:

HAPPY   ENERGETIC   CALM   STRESSED   SAD   TIRED

❯ THOUGHT LOG: ❮

WHAT WAS ON MY MIND TODAY? _____

_____

_____

_____

_____

HOW MIGHT I REFRAME THOSE THOUGHTS? _____

_____

_____

_____

_____

❯ TRIGGER TRACKER: ❮

DID SOMETHING TRIGGER MY ANXIETY TODAY? _____

_____

_____

_____

_____

HOW DID I RESPOND? _____

_____

_____

_____

_____

ACCOMPLISHMENTS/WINS:

1	2	3

SELF-CARE:

- ☐ DID I SLEEP WELL?
- ☐ DID I GET EXERCISE?
- ☐ DID I GET FRESH AIR?
- ☐ DID I MEDITATE?
- ☐ DID I EAT NOURISHING FOODS?

DAILY GRATITUDE:

1. _____
2. _____
3. _____
4. _____
5. _____

SOMETHING THAT
MADE ME HAPPY TODAY:

DATE _____

OVERALL MOOD:

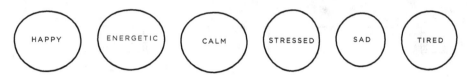

(HAPPY) (ENERGETIC) (CALM) (STRESSED) (SAD) (TIRED)

➤ THOUGHT LOG: ❰

WHAT WAS ON MY MIND TODAY? _____
_____
_____
_____

HOW MIGHT I REFRAME THOSE THOUGHTS? _____
_____
_____
_____

➤ TRIGGER TRACKER: ❰

DID SOMETHING TRIGGER MY ANXIETY TODAY? _____
_____
_____
_____

HOW DID I RESPOND? _____
_____
_____
_____

DAY: 2

ACCOMPLISHMENTS/WINS:

1	2	3

SELF-CARE:

- ☐ DID I SLEEP WELL?
- ☐ DID I GET EXERCISE?
- ☐ DID I GET FRESH AIR?
- ☐ DID I MEDITATE?
- ☐ DID I EAT NOURISHING FOODS?

DAILY GRATITUDE:

1. _____
2. _____
3. _____
4. _____
5. _____

SOMETHING THAT
MADE ME HAPPY TODAY:

DATE _____

OVERALL MOOD:

(HAPPY) (ENERGETIC) (CALM) (STRESSED) (SAD) (TIRED)

➤ THOUGHT LOG: ❰

WHAT WAS ON MY MIND TODAY? _____

_____

_____

_____

_____

HOW MIGHT I REFRAME THOSE THOUGHTS? _____

_____

_____

_____

_____

➤ TRIGGER TRACKER: ❰

DID SOMETHING TRIGGER MY ANXIETY TODAY? _____

_____

_____

_____

HOW DID I RESPOND? _____

_____

_____

_____

_____

ACCOMPLISHMENTS/WINS:

1	2	3

SELF-CARE:

- ☐ DID I SLEEP WELL?
- ☐ DID I GET EXERCISE?
- ☐ DID I GET FRESH AIR?
- ☐ DID I MEDITATE?
- ☐ DID I EAT NOURISHING FOODS?

DAILY GRATITUDE:

1. _____
2. _____
3. _____
4. _____
5. _____

SOMETHING THAT MADE ME HAPPY TODAY:

DATE_____

OVERALL MOOD:

(HAPPY) (ENERGETIC) (CALM) (STRESSED) (SAD) (TIRED)

❯ THOUGHT LOG: ❮

WHAT WAS ON MY MIND TODAY? _____

_____

_____

_____

_____

HOW MIGHT I REFRAME THOSE THOUGHTS? _____

_____

_____

_____

_____

❯ TRIGGER TRACKER: ❮

DID SOMETHING TRIGGER MY ANXIETY TODAY? _____

_____

_____

_____

_____

HOW DID I RESPOND? _____

_____

_____

_____

_____

DAY: 4

ACCOMPLISHMENTS/WINS:

1	2	3

SELF-CARE:

☐ DID I SLEEP WELL?

☐ DID I GET EXERCISE?

☐ DID I GET FRESH AIR?

☐ DID I MEDITATE?

☐ DID I EAT NOURISHING FOODS?

DAILY GRATITUDE:

1. _____

2. _____

3. _____

4. _____

5. _____

SOMETHING THAT
MADE ME HAPPY TODAY:

DATE _____

OVERALL MOOD:

(HAPPY) (ENERGETIC) (CALM) (STRESSED) (SAD) (TIRED)

> **THOUGHT LOG:** <

WHAT WAS ON MY MIND TODAY? _____
_____
_____
_____

HOW MIGHT I REFRAME THOSE THOUGHTS? _____
_____
_____
_____

> **TRIGGER TRACKER:** <

DID SOMETHING TRIGGER MY ANXIETY TODAY? _____
_____
_____
_____

HOW DID I RESPOND? _____
_____
_____
_____

DAY: 5

ACCOMPLISHMENTS/WINS:

1	2	3

SELF-CARE:

☐ DID I SLEEP WELL?

☐ DID I GET EXERCISE?

☐ DID I GET FRESH AIR?

☐ DID I MEDITATE?

☐ DID I EAT NOURISHING FOODS?

DAILY GRATITUDE:

1. _____

2. _____

3. _____

4. _____

5. _____

**SOMETHING THAT
MADE ME HAPPY TODAY:**

DATE _____

OVERALL MOOD:

(HAPPY) (ENERGETIC) (CALM) (STRESSED) (SAD) (TIRED)

❯ THOUGHT LOG: ❮

WHAT WAS ON MY MIND TODAY? _____

_____

_____

_____

HOW MIGHT I REFRAME THOSE THOUGHTS? _____

_____

_____

_____

❯ TRIGGER TRACKER: ❮

DID SOMETHING TRIGGER MY ANXIETY TODAY? _____

_____

_____

_____

HOW DID I RESPOND? _____

_____

_____

_____

DAY: 6

ACCOMPLISHMENTS/WINS:

1	2	3

SELF-CARE:

☐ DID I SLEEP WELL?

☐ DID I GET EXERCISE?

☐ DID I GET FRESH AIR?

☐ DID I MEDITATE?

☐ DID I EAT NOURISHING FOODS?

DAILY GRATITUDE:

1. _____

2. _____

3. _____

4. _____

5. _____

SOMETHING THAT
MADE ME HAPPY TODAY:

DATE_____

OVERALL MOOD:

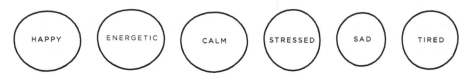

(HAPPY) (ENERGETIC) (CALM) (STRESSED) (SAD) (TIRED)

➤ THOUGHT LOG: ❮

WHAT WAS ON MY MIND TODAY? _____

_____

_____

_____

HOW MIGHT I REFRAME THOSE THOUGHTS? _____

_____

_____

_____

➤ TRIGGER TRACKER: ❮

DID SOMETHING TRIGGER MY ANXIETY TODAY? _____

_____

_____

_____

HOW DID I RESPOND? _____

_____

_____

_____

ACCOMPLISHMENTS/WINS:

1

2

3

SELF-CARE:

☐ DID I SLEEP WELL?

☐ DID I GET EXERCISE?

☐ DID I GET FRESH AIR?

☐ DID I MEDITATE?

☐ DID I EAT NOURISHING FOODS?

DAILY GRATITUDE:

1. _____

2. _____

3. _____

4. _____

5. _____

SOMETHING THAT MADE ME HAPPY TODAY:

WEEKLY FEAR-SETTING:

WHAT AM I WORRIED ABOUT RIGHT NOW? _____

_____

_____

_____

HOW LIKELY IS IT FOR THIS TO ACTUALLY OCCUR? THINK OF YOUR
PAST EXPERIENCES AND WRITE ANY EXAMPLES HERE. _____

_____

_____

_____

WHAT'S THE WORST-CASE SCENARIO?

% CHANCE OF THAT HAPPENING? _____

WHAT'S THE BEST-CASE SCENARIO?

% CHANCE OF THAT HAPPENING? _____

WHAT'S THE MOST LIKELY SCENARIO?

% CHANCE OF THAT HAPPENING? _____

HAPPY HABIT TRACKER:

HABIT TRACKER:	S	M	T	W	T	F	S
	☐	☐	☐	☐	☐	☐	☐
	☐	☐	☐	☐	☐	☐	☐
	☐	☐	☐	☐	☐	☐	☐
	☐	☐	☐	☐	☐	☐	☐
	☐	☐	☐	☐	☐	☐	☐
	☐	☐	☐	☐	☐	☐	☐
	☐	☐	☐	☐	☐	☐	☐
	☐	☐	☐	☐	☐	☐	☐
	☐	☐	☐	☐	☐	☐	☐
	☐	☐	☐	☐	☐	☐	☐
	☐	☐	☐	☐	☐	☐	☐
	☐	☐	☐	☐	☐	☐	☐
	☐	☐	☐	☐	☐	☐	☐
	☐	☐	☐	☐	☐	☐	☐
	☐	☐	☐	☐	☐	☐	☐
	☐	☐	☐	☐	☐	☐	☐

THERAPY REFLECTIONS:

TOPIC WE DISCUSSED:
....

HOW I FEEL ABOUT IT:
....

TAKEAWAYS:
....

FOR NEXT TIME:
....

WEEK 12:

DATE _____

OVERALL MOOD:

(HAPPY)   (ENERGETIC)   (CALM)   (STRESSED)   (SAD)   (TIRED)

❯ THOUGHT LOG: ❮

WHAT WAS ON MY MIND TODAY? _____

_____

_____

_____

_____

HOW MIGHT I REFRAME THOSE THOUGHTS? _____

_____

_____

_____

_____

❯ TRIGGER TRACKER: ❮

DID SOMETHING TRIGGER MY ANXIETY TODAY? _____

_____

_____

_____

_____

HOW DID I RESPOND? _____

_____

_____

_____

_____

DAY: 1

ACCOMPLISHMENTS/WINS:

1

2

3

SELF-CARE:

☐ DID I SLEEP WELL?

☐ DID I GET EXERCISE?

☐ DID I GET FRESH AIR?

☐ DID I MEDITATE?

☐ DID I EAT NOURISHING
FOODS?

DAILY GRATITUDE:

1. _____

2. _____

3. _____

4. _____

5. _____

SOMETHING THAT
MADE ME HAPPY TODAY:

DATE_____

OVERALL MOOD:

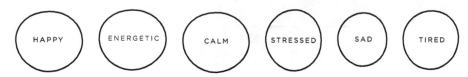

(HAPPY) (ENERGETIC) (CALM) (STRESSED) (SAD) (TIRED)

➤ THOUGHT LOG: ◄

WHAT WAS ON MY MIND TODAY? _____
_____
_____
_____

HOW MIGHT I REFRAME THOSE THOUGHTS? _____
_____
_____
_____

➤ TRIGGER TRACKER: ◄

DID SOMETHING TRIGGER MY ANXIETY TODAY? _____
_____
_____
_____

HOW DID I RESPOND? _____
_____
_____
_____

ACCOMPLISHMENTS/WINS:

1	2	3

SELF-CARE:

- ☐ DID I SLEEP WELL?
- ☐ DID I GET EXERCISE?
- ☐ DID I GET FRESH AIR?
- ☐ DID I MEDITATE?
- ☐ DID I EAT NOURISHING FOODS?

DAILY GRATITUDE:

1. _____
2. _____
3. _____
4. _____
5. _____

SOMETHING THAT
MADE ME HAPPY TODAY:

DATE _____

OVERALL MOOD:

(HAPPY) (ENERGETIC) (CALM) (STRESSED) (SAD) (TIRED)

❯ THOUGHT LOG: ❮

WHAT WAS ON MY MIND TODAY? _____

_____

_____

_____

HOW MIGHT I REFRAME THOSE THOUGHTS? _____

_____

_____

_____

_____

❯ TRIGGER TRACKER: ❮

DID SOMETHING TRIGGER MY ANXIETY TODAY? _____

_____

_____

_____

HOW DID I RESPOND? _____

_____

_____

_____

_____

ACCOMPLISHMENTS/WINS:

1	2	3

SELF-CARE:

- ☐ DID I SLEEP WELL?
- ☐ DID I GET EXERCISE?
- ☐ DID I GET FRESH AIR?
- ☐ DID I MEDITATE?
- ☐ DID I EAT NOURISHING FOODS?

DAILY GRATITUDE:

1. _____
2. _____
3. _____
4. _____
5. _____

SOMETHING THAT
MADE ME HAPPY TODAY:

DATE _____

OVERALL MOOD:

(HAPPY) (ENERGETIC) (CALM) (STRESSED) (SAD) (TIRED)

> **THOUGHT LOG:** ◄

WHAT WAS ON MY MIND TODAY? _____

_____

_____

_____

HOW MIGHT I REFRAME THOSE THOUGHTS? _____

_____

_____

_____

_____

> **TRIGGER TRACKER:** ◄

DID SOMETHING TRIGGER MY ANXIETY TODAY? _____

_____

_____

_____

HOW DID I RESPOND? _____

_____

_____

_____

ACCOMPLISHMENTS/WINS:

1	2	3

SELF-CARE:

- ☐ DID I SLEEP WELL?
- ☐ DID I GET EXERCISE?
- ☐ DID I GET FRESH AIR?
- ☐ DID I MEDITATE?
- ☐ DID I EAT NOURISHING FOODS?

DAILY GRATITUDE:

1. _____
2. _____
3. _____
4. _____
5. _____

SOMETHING THAT
MADE ME HAPPY TODAY:

DATE _____

OVERALL MOOD:

(HAPPY) (ENERGETIC) (CALM) (STRESSED) (SAD) (TIRED)

❯ THOUGHT LOG: ❮

WHAT WAS ON MY MIND TODAY? _____
_____
_____
_____

HOW MIGHT I REFRAME THOSE THOUGHTS? _____
_____
_____
_____

❯ TRIGGER TRACKER: ❮

DID SOMETHING TRIGGER MY ANXIETY TODAY? _____
_____
_____
_____

HOW DID I RESPOND? _____
_____
_____
_____

ACCOMPLISHMENTS/WINS:

1

2

3

SELF-CARE:

☐ DID I SLEEP WELL?

☐ DID I GET EXERCISE?

☐ DID I GET FRESH AIR?

☐ DID I MEDITATE?

☐ DID I EAT NOURISHING
FOODS?

DAILY GRATITUDE:

1. _____

2. _____

3. _____

4. _____

5. _____

SOMETHING THAT
MADE ME HAPPY TODAY:

DATE _____

OVERALL MOOD:

(HAPPY)   (ENERGETIC)   (CALM)   (STRESSED)   (SAD)   (TIRED)

❯ THOUGHT LOG: ❮

WHAT WAS ON MY MIND TODAY? _____

_____

_____

_____

HOW MIGHT I REFRAME THOSE THOUGHTS? _____

_____

_____

_____

❯ TRIGGER TRACKER: ❮

DID SOMETHING TRIGGER MY ANXIETY TODAY? _____

_____

_____

_____

HOW DID I RESPOND? _____

_____

_____

_____

DAY: 6

ACCOMPLISHMENTS/WINS:

```
┌─────────────┐  ┌─────────────┐  ┌─────────────┐
│ 1 │         │  │ 2 │         │  │ 3 │         │
│   └         │  │   └         │  │   └         │
│             │  │             │  │             │
│             │  │             │  │             │
│             │  │             │  │             │
│             │  │             │  │             │
│             │  │             │  │             │
└─────────────┘  └─────────────┘  └─────────────┘
```

SELF-CARE:

☐ DID I SLEEP WELL?

☐ DID I GET EXERCISE?

☐ DID I GET FRESH AIR?

☐ DID I MEDITATE?

☐ DID I EAT NOURISHING
   FOODS?

DAILY GRATITUDE:

1. _____

2. _____

3. _____

4. _____

5. _____

SOMETHING THAT
MADE ME HAPPY TODAY:

DATE_____

OVERALL MOOD:

HAPPY   ENERGETIC   CALM   STRESSED   SAD   TIRED

➤ THOUGHT LOG: ❮

WHAT WAS ON MY MIND TODAY? _____
_____
_____
_____
_____

HOW MIGHT I REFRAME THOSE THOUGHTS? _____
_____
_____
_____
_____

➤ TRIGGER TRACKER: ❮

DID SOMETHING TRIGGER MY ANXIETY TODAY? _____
_____
_____
_____
_____

HOW DID I RESPOND? _____
_____
_____
_____
_____

ACCOMPLISHMENTS/WINS:

1	2	3

SELF-CARE:

☐ DID I SLEEP WELL?

☐ DID I GET EXERCISE?

☐ DID I GET FRESH AIR?

☐ DID I MEDITATE?

☐ DID I EAT NOURISHING FOODS?

DAILY GRATITUDE:

1. _____

2. _____

3. _____

4. _____

5. _____

SOMETHING THAT
MADE ME HAPPY TODAY:

WEEKLY FEAR-SETTING:

WHAT AM I WORRIED ABOUT RIGHT NOW? _____

_____

_____

_____

HOW LIKELY IS IT FOR THIS TO ACTUALLY OCCUR? THINK OF YOUR
PAST EXPERIENCES AND WRITE ANY EXAMPLES HERE. _____

_____

_____

_____

WHAT'S THE WORST-CASE SCENARIO?

% CHANCE OF THAT HAPPENING? _____

WHAT'S THE BEST-CASE SCENARIO?

% CHANCE OF THAT HAPPENING? _____

WHAT'S THE MOST LIKELY SCENARIO?

% CHANCE OF THAT HAPPENING? _____

HAPPY HABIT TRACKER:

HABIT TRACKER:	S	M	T	W	T	F	S
	☐	☐	☐	☐	☐	☐	☐
	☐	☐	☐	☐	☐	☐	☐
	☐	☐	☐	☐	☐	☐	☐
	☐	☐	☐	☐	☐	☐	☐
	☐	☐	☐	☐	☐	☐	☐
	☐	☐	☐	☐	☐	☐	☐
	☐	☐	☐	☐	☐	☐	☐
	☐	☐	☐	☐	☐	☐	☐
	☐	☐	☐	☐	☐	☐	☐
	☐	☐	☐	☐	☐	☐	☐
	☐	☐	☐	☐	☐	☐	☐
	☐	☐	☐	☐	☐	☐	☐
	☐	☐	☐	☐	☐	☐	☐
	☐	☐	☐	☐	☐	☐	☐
	☐	☐	☐	☐	☐	☐	☐
	☐	☐	☐	☐	☐	☐	☐

THERAPY REFLECTIONS:

TOPIC WE DISCUSSED:
....

HOW I FEEL ABOUT IT:
....

TAKEAWAYS:
....

FOR NEXT TIME:
....

MONTH:_____

MONTHLY CHECK-IN:

HOW I FEEL ABOUT THIS MONTH OVERALL:

WHAT CHANGED SINCE LAST MONTH?

ACCOMPLISHMENTS:

1

2

3

THINGS I WANT TO IMPROVE OR ACCOMPLISH NEXT MONTH:

MEASURE YOUR SATISFACTION:

VERY UNSATISFIED   INDIFFERENT   VERY SATISFIED

O———————————O———————————O

0   1   2   3   4   5   6

HOUSING SITUATION: _____   ENERGY/MOTIVATION: _____

FAMILY: _____   WORK/LIFE BALANCE: _____

FRIENDS: _____   OVERALL HEALTH: _____

SPOUSE/PARTNER: _____   DOCTOR/THERAPIST: _____

SENSE OF COMMUNITY: _____   MONEY/FINANCES: _____

HOBBIES/ACTIVITIES: _____   LIFE PURPOSE: _____

SCHOOL/WORK: _____   QUALITY OF LIFE: _____

3 AREAS OF MY LIFE WHERE I'D LIKE TO IMPROVE:

1. _____
2. _____
3. _____

3 IDEAS FOR HOW I CAN MAKE PROGRESS:

1. _____
2. _____
3. _____

9 781952 676000